Ace's

ITALIAN
PHRASE BOOK
& DICTIONARY
for Travelers

Charles A. Hughes

ace books

A Division of Charter Communications Inc.
A GROSSET & DUNLAP COMPANY
51 Madison Avenue
New York, New York 10010

Copyright © 1971 Grosset & Dunlap, Inc.
All Rights Reserved
ISBN: 0-441-37488-3
First Ace Printing: June 1981
Published simultaneously in Canada
Printed in the United States of America

Cover photo by FOUR BY FIVE

CONTENTS

INTRODUCTION

In this phrase book for travel in Italy, we have tried to incorporate features that will make it convenient and easy for you to use in actual situations. Every phrase and word is translated into proper Italian and then respelled to guide you in its pronunciation.

The book is also "programmed" to help you with two of the basic problems of the novice in a language — an inability to comprehend the spoken word and a certain hesitancy in speaking out. To solve the first problem, questions have been avoided, to the extent possible, in the phrases. When they could not be avoided, they have been worded so that a yes or no answer may be expected. And sometimes, when even this solution is impossible, the anticipated answer is given. To solve the problem of hesitancy, the contents of the book have been arranged so that a minimal command of basic phrases, salutations, weather, numbers-time, statements of need and desire, may be acquired in the first sections. The pronunciation guides printed under the Italian translations should also give you confidence that you will be understood. If your listener should indicate that he doesn't understand, merely try again. A slight mispronunciation is no embarrassment.

Finally, to aid you in finding a phrase that you wish to use, the Dictionary has been partially indexed. The Dictionary itself is comprehensive enough so that you will not lack the basic words for any usual situation.

TIPS ON PRONUNCIATION AND ACCENT

The pronunciation of each word in this phrase book is indicated by a respelling that approximates the sounds of Italian, according to the following system:

The vowels:

ah	Pronounced like "a" in f*a*ther
eh	Pronounced like "ay" in m*ay*be
e	Pronounced like "e" in m*e*t
ee	Pronounced like "ee" in s*ee*n
o	Pronounced like "o" in b*o*y
oh	Pronounced like "o" in *o*ver
oo	Pronounced like "oo" in s*oo*n
ah-ee	Pronounced like the pronoun *I* or the word *eye*
ow	Pronounced like "ow" in n*ow*
wah	Pronounced like "wa" in *wa*ter
woh	Pronounced like "wo" in *wo*n't
oy	Pronounced like "oy" in b*oy*

Consonants are sounded approximately as in English, with these exceptions:

"c" before "a," "o" and "u" sounds like "c" in *c*an; it is represented in the pronunciations by "k."

"c" before "e" and "i" sounds like "ch" in *ch*urch.

"ch" sounds like "k" in s*k*ate.

"g" before "a," "o" and "u" sounds like "g" in *g*o.

"g" before "e" and "i" sounds like "g" in *g*em or "j" in *j*oy.

"gh" sounds like "g" in *g*o.

"gl" sounds like "lli" in mi*lli*on.

"gn" sounds like "ny" in ca*ny*on.

"h" is always silent.

"r" is always trilled.

"s" between vowels and before voiced consonants sounds like "z" in *z*ebra.

"s" when it is initial, or is doubled in writing, or comes before voiceless consonants sounds like "ss" in mi*ss*.

"z" sounds like "ts" in ca*ts* or like "dz" in a*dz*e.

All consonants written double in Italian are pronounced twice as long as their single counterparts.

In the pronunciations, the stress or main accent in a word is indicated by an accent mark (′) after the stressed syllable.

brother, fratello *frah-tel′-loh*
four, quattro *kwaht′-troh*
city, città *cheet-tah′*
lightning, fulmine *fool′-mee-neh*

Salutations and Greetings

Even before you learn anything else in a foreign language, you will want to learn how to greet people. Here are some short expressions that you will find easy to learn and to use when you meet people in a foreign land or along the way, perhaps on the ship or the plane.

Good morning.
Buon giorno.
Bwon jor'-noh

Good day.
Buon giorno
Bwon jor'-noh.

Good afternoon.
Buon giorno.
Bwon jor'-noh.

Good evening.
Buona sera.
Bwoh'-nah seh'-rah.

Good-bye.
Addio.
Ad-dee'-yoh.

Good-night.
Buona notte.
Bwoh'-nah not'-teh.

How are you?
Come sta?
Ko'-meh stah?

Well, thank you. And you?
Bene, grazie. E Lei?
Beh'-neh, grah'-tsee-yeh. Eh leh'-ee?

How is Mr. . . . ?
Come sta il signor . . . ?
Ko'-meh stah eel seen-yor' . . ?

How is Mrs. . . . ?
Come sta la signora . . . ?
Ko'-meh stah lah seen-yoh'-rah . . . ?

Is Miss . . . well?
Sta bene la signorina . . . ?
Stah beh'-neh lah seen-yoh-ree'-nah . . . ?

May I present my wife?
Posso presentare mia moglie?
Pos'-soh preh-zen-tah'-reh mee'-yah mo'-lyeh?

This is my husband.
Questo è mio marito.
Kwehs'-toh e mee'-yoh mah-ree'-toh.

Pleased to meet you.
Piacere di conoscerla.
Pyah-che'-reh dee ko-no'-sher-lah.

This is my friend.
Questo è il mio amico (m).
*Kwehs'-toh e eel mee'-yoh
  ah-mee'-koh.*

This is my friend.
Questa è la mia amica (f).
*Kwehs'-tah e lah mee'-yah
  ah-mee'-kah.*

This is my mother and my father.
Questa è mia madre e questo è mio padre.
Kwehs'-tah e mee'-yah mah'-dreh eh kwes'-toh e mee'-yoh pah'-dreh.

This is my sister and my brother.
Questa è mia sorella e questo è mio fratello.
Kwes'-tah e mee'-yah so-rel'-lah eh kwes'-toh e mee'-yoh frah-tel'-loh.

Is this your daughter?
È questa Sua figlia?
E kwes'-tah soo'-ah feel'-yah?

Is this your son?
È questo Suo figlio?
E kwes'-toh soo-oh feel'-yoh?

I hope that we will meet again.
Spero che ci incontriamo di nuovo.
Spe'-roh keh chee een-kon-tree-yah'-moh dee nwoh'-voh.

I'll be seeing you.
Arrivederci.
Ahr-ree-veh-der'-chee.

I'll see you tomorrow.
Ci vediamo domani.
Chee veh-dee-yah'-moh doh-mah'-nee.

Excuse me.
Mi scusi.
Mee skoo'-zee.

Pardon me.
Scusi.
Skoo'-zee.

I'm very sorry.
Mi dispiace molto. / Mi rincresce molto.
Mee dees-pyah'-cheh mol'-toh. / Mee reen-kre'-sheh mol'-toh

Don't mention it.
Non c'è di che.
Non che dee keh.

You're welcome.
Prego.
Preh'-goh.

Please.
Per favore. / Per piacere.
*Per fah-voh'-reh. / Per pyah-
cheh'-reh.*

With pleasure.
Con piacere.
Kon pyah-cheh'-reh.

Good luck!
Buona fortuna.
Bwoh'-nah for-too'-nah!

The Weather

The weather is one thing everyone has in common, and it is a universal topic of conversation. The phrases given here — combined with a bit of added vocabulary — are easily mastered.

It's nice weather today.
Oggi fa bel tempo.
Oj'-jee fah bel tem'-poh.

It's bad weather today.
Oggi fa brutto tempo.
Oj'-jee fah broot'-toh tem'-poh.

It's cold.
Fa freddo.
Fah frehd'-doh.

It's warm.
Fa caldo.
Fah kahl'-doh.

Is it raining?
Piove?
Pyo'-veh?

Yes, it's raining.
Sì, piove.
See, pyo'-veh.

No, it's not raining.
No, non piove.
Noh, non pyo'-veh.

It's snowing.
Nevica.
Neh'-vee-kah.

It rains (snows) here every day.
Qui piove (nevica) tutti i giorni.
Kwee pyo'-veh (neh'-vee-kah) toot'-tee ee jor'-nee.

It's beginning to rain (to snow).
Comincia a piovere (nevicare).
Ko-meen'-chah ah pyo'-veh-reh (neh-vee-kah'-reh).

It often rains (snows) here.
Qui piove (nevica) spesso.
Kwee pyo'-veh (neh'-vee-kah) spes'-soh.

It will rain (snow) tomorrow.
Domani pioverà (nevicherà).
Doh-mah'-nee pyo-ve-rah' (neh-vee-ke-rah').

It rained (snowed) yesterday.
Ha piovuto (nevicato) ieri.
Ah pyo-voo'-toh (neh-vee-kah'-toh) ye'-ree.

It has stopped raining (snowing).
Ha cessato di piovere (nevicare).
Ah ches-sah'-toh dee pyo'-ve-reh (neh-vee-kah'-reh).

It's windy.
Tira vento.
Tee'-rah ven'-toh.

There's a lot of fog.
C'è molta nebbia.
Che mol'-tah nehb'-byah.

The sun is rising.
Il sole si leva.
Eel so'-leh see leh'-vah.

The sun is setting.
Il sole tramonta.
Eel so'-leh trah-mon'-tah.

How is the weather?
Che tempo fa?
Keh tem'-poh fah?

I need an umbrella.
Ho bisogno d'un ombrello.
Oh bee-zo'-nyoh doon om-brel'-loh.

I see . . .	I like . . .	I'm afraid of . .
Vedo . . .	Mi piace . . .	Ho paura di . . .
Veh'-doh . . .	*Mee pyah'-cheh*...	*Ah pah-oo'-rah dee* . . .

the rain.
la pioggia.
lah pyoj'-jah.

the wind.
il vento.
eel ven'-toh.

the snow.
la neve.
lah neh'-veh.

the ice.
il ghiaccio.
eel gyahch'-choh.

the sky.
il cielo.
eel chyeh'-loh.

the sun.
il sole.
eel soh'-leh.

the moon.
la luna.
la loo'-nah.

the stars.
le stelle.
leh stel'-leh.

a star.
una stella.
oo'-nah stel'-lah.

a rainbow.
un arcobaleno.
oon ahr-koh-bah-leh'-noh.

a cloud.
una nuvola.
oo'-nah noo'-voh-lah.

the clouds.
le nuvole.
leh noo'-voh-leh.

the lightning.
il fulmine, i lampi.
eel fool'-mee-neh, ee lahm'-pee.

the thunder.
il tuono.
eel twoh'-noh.

the storm.
la tempesta, il temporale.
lah tem-pe'-stah, eel tem-poh-rah'-leh.

Will it be cool there?
Farà fresco là?
Fah-rah' fres'-koh lah?

Will it be damp there?
Ci sarà umidità?
Chee sah-rah' oo-mee-dee-tah'?

Should I take a sweater?
Dovrei prendere un maglione?
Dov-reh'-ee pren'-deh-reh oon mah-lyoh'-neh?

a jacket?
una giacca?
oo'-nah jahk'-kah?

a raincoat?
un impermeabile?
oon eem-per-meh-yah'-bee-leh?

It's lightning.
Lampeggia.
Lahm-pej'-jah.

It's thundering.
Tuona.
Twoh'-nah.

Warm weather.
Tempo caldo.
Tem'-poh kahl'-doh.

Cold weather.
Tempo freddo.
Tem'-poh frehd'-doh.

Warm water.
Acqua calda.
Ahk'-kwah kahl'-dah.

Hot water.
Acqua caldissima.
Ahk'-kwah kahl-dees'-see-mah.

Cold water.
Acqua fredda.
Ahk'-kwah frehd'-dah.

General Expressions

In this section you will find the most useful expressions — the ones you will use over and over again. They are the phrases that you should have on the tip of the tongue, ready for immediate use — particularly those that express desire or volition. Here they have been kept short for easy acquisition and speedy communication. You will see them appear again and again in other sections of this book, where they are used in particular situations.

What is your name?
Come si chiama Lei?
Ko'-meh see kyah'-mah leh'-ee?

My name is . . .
Mi chiamo . . .
Mee kyah'-moh . . .

What is his (her) name?
Come si chiama lui (lei)?
Ko'-meh see kyah'-mah loo'-ee (leh'-ee)?

I don't know.
Non lo so.
Non loh soh.

His (her) name is . . .
Si chiama . . .
See kyah'-mah . . .

Do you know him (her)?
Lo (La) conosce?
Loh (lah) ko-no'-sheh?

Yes, I know him (her).
Sí, lo (la) conosco.
See, loh (lah) ko-nos'-koh.

No, I don't know him (her).
No, non lo (la) conosco.
Noh, non loh (lah) ko-nos'-koh.

I know you.
La conosco.
Lah ko-nos'-koh.

Where do you live?
Dove abita Lei?
Do'-veh ah'-bee-tah leh'-ee?

I live here.
Abito qui.
Ah'-bee-toh kwee.

At which hotel are you staying?
A quale albergo scende?
Ah kwah'-leh ahl-ber'-goh shen'-deh?

She's a beautiful woman.
È una bella donna.
E oo'-nah bel'-lah don'-nah.

She's a pretty girl.
È una ragazza graziosa.
E oo'-nah rah-gaht'-tsah grah-tsyoh'-zah.

He's a handsome man.
È un bell'uomo.
E oon bel-lwoh'-moh.

I love you.
Ti amo.
Tee ah'-moh.

I love her.
L'amo.
Lah'-moh.

I love him.
Lo amo.
Loh ah'-moh.

Do you know where he lives?
Sa dove lui abita?
Sah do'-veh loo'-ee ah'-bee-tah?

Do you speak English?
Parla Lei inglese?
Pahr'-lah leh'-ee een-gleh'-zeh?

Please say it in English.
Lo dica in inglese, per favore.
Loh dee'-kah een een-gleh'-zeh, per fah-voh'-reh.

Is there anyone here who speaks English?
C'è qualcuno qui che parla inglese?
Che kwahl-koo'-noh kwee keh pahr'-lah een-gleh'-zeh?

Do you understand?
Capisce?
Kah-pee'-sheh?

Yes, I understand.
Sì, capisco.
See, kah-pees'-koh.

No, I don't understand.
No, non capisco.
Noh, non kah-pees'-koh.

I understand a little.
Capisco un poco.
Kah-pees'-koh oon poh'-koh.

I don't understand everything.
Non capisco tutto.
Non kah-pees'-koh toot'-toh.

Please speak more slowly.
Parli più lentamente (adagio), per favore.
Pahr'-lee pyoo len-tah-men'-teh (ah-dah'-joh) per fah-voh'-reh.

Please repeat.
Ripeta, per favore.
Ree-peh'-tah, per fah-voh'-reh.

What did you say?
Che cosa ha detto?
Keh ko'-zah ah det'-toh?

How do you say that in Italian?
Come si dice questo in italiano?
Ko'-meh see dee'-cheh kwes'-toh een ee-tah-lyah'-noh?

What does that mean?
Che significa questo?
*Keh see-nyee'-fee-kah
kwes'-toh?*

What do you mean?
Che vuol dire?
Keh vwohl dee'-reh?

You are right (wrong).
Lei ha ragione (torto).
*Leh'-ee ah rah-joh'-neh
(tor'-toh).*

He is right (wrong).
Lui ha ragione (torto).
*Loo'-ee ah rah-joh'-neh
(tor'-toh).*

Without doubt.
Senza dubbio.
Sehn'-tsah doob'-byoh.

Where are you going?
Dove va Lei? Dove va?
Do'-veh vah leh'-ee?

Where is he going?
Dove va lui? Dove va?
Do'-veh vah loo'-ee?

Where are we going?
Dove andiamo?
Do'-veh ahn-dyah'-moh?

I will wait here.
Aspetterò qui.
Ah-spet-te-roh' kwee.

How long must I wait?
Quanto tempo devo aspettare?
Kwahn'-toh tem'-poh deh'-voh ah-spet-tah'-reh?

Wait here until I come back.
Aspetti qui finchè torni.
Ah-spet'-tee kwee feen-keh' tor'-nee.

Come here.
Venga qua.
Ven'-gah kwah.

Is it near here?
È qui vicino?
E kwee vee-chee'-noh?

Come in.
Avanti.
Ah-vahn'-tee.

Is it far from here?
È lontano da qui?
E lon-tah'-noh dah kwee?

Bring me . . .
Mi porti . . .
Mee por'-tee . . .

Tell me . .
Mi dica . . .
Mee dee'-kah

Give me . . .
Mi dia . . .
Mee dee'-yah . . .

Show me . . .
Mi mostri . . .
Mee mos'-tree . . .

Send me . . .
Mi mandi . . .
Mee mahn'-dee . . .

Write to me . . .
Mi scriva . . .
Mee skree'-vah . .

I need . . .
Ho bisogno di . . .
Oh bee-zo'-nyoh dee . . .

I would like . . .
Vorrei . . .
Vor-reh'-ee . . .

I want . . .
Voglio (Desidero) . . .
Vo'-lyoh (deh-zee'-de-roh) . . .

I don't want . . .
Non voglio (desidero) . .
Non vo'-lyoh (deh-zee'-de-roh) . . .

I can do that.
Posso fare questo.
Pos'-soh fah'-reh kwes'-toh.

I cannot do that.
Non posso fare questo.
Non pos'-soh fah'-reh kwes'-toh.

Have you . . . ?
Ha Lei . . . ?
Ah leh'-ee . . . ?

Are you . . . ?
È Lei . . . ?
E leh'-ee . . . ?

Where is . . . ?
Dov'è . . . ?
Do-ve' . . . ?

Where are . . . ?
Dove sono . . . ?
Do'-veh soh'-noh . . . ?

It's possible.
È possibile.
E pos-see'-bee-leh.

It's impossible.
E impossibile.
È eem-pos-see'-bee-leh.

Emergencies

You will probably never need to use any of the brief cries, entreaties, or commands that appear here, but accidents do happen, items may be mislaid or stolen, and mistakes do occur. If an emergency does arise, it will probably be covered by one of these expressions.

Help!
Aiuto! Al soccorso!
Ah-yoo'-toh! Ahl sok-kor'-soh!

Help me!
Mi aiuti!
Mee ah-yoo'-tee!

There has been an accident!
C'è stato un incidente!
Che stah'-toh oon een-chee-den'-teh!

Stop!
Alt! Fermate!
Ahlt! Fer-mah'-teh!

Hurry up!
Faccia presto!
Fahch'-chah pres'-toh!

Look out!
Attenzione!
Aht-ten-tsyoh'-neh!

Send for a doctor!
Faccia venire un medico!
*Fahch'-chah veh-nee'-reh
oon meh'-dee-koh!*

Poison!
Veleno!
Veh-leh'-noh!

Fire!
Fuoco!
Fwoh'-koh!

Police!
Polizia!
Poh-lee-tsee'-yah!

What happened?
Che cosa è successo?
*Keh ko'-zah e sooch-
chehs'-soh?*

What's the matter?
Che c'è?
Keh che?

Don't worry!
Non si preoccupi!
Non see preh-ok'-koo-pee!

I missed the train (bus) (plane).
Ho perduto il treno (autobus) (aeroplano).
*Oh per-doo'-toh eel treh'-noh (ow-toh-boos') (ah-eh-roh-
plah'-noh).*

I've been robbed!
Sono stato derubato!
Soh'-noh stah'-toh deh-roo-bah'-toh!

That man stole my money!
Quell'uomo mi ha rubato il denaro!
Kwel-lwoh'-moh mee ah roo-bah'-toh eel deh-nah'-roh!

Call the police!
Chiami la polizia!
Kyah'-mee lah poh-lee-tsee'-yah!

I have lost my money!
Ho perduto il mio denaro!
Oh per-doo'-toh eel mee-yoh deh-nah'-roh!

I have lost my passport!
Ho perduto il mio passaporte!
Oh per-doo'-toh eel mee'-yoh pahs-sah-por'-teh!

It's an American (British) passport.
È un passaporte americano (inglese).
E oon pahs-sah-por'-teh ah-meh-ree-kah'-noh (een-gleh'-zeh).

Stay where you are!   **Don't move!**
Rimanete dove siete!   Non si muova!
Ree-mah-neh'-teh do'-veh   *Non see mwoh'-vah!*
sye'-teh!

direción de la hotel
no me dea (dare)
passyports Americanos,

Stayd Aug 4.

Signs and Notices

You could probably get along in a foreign land without speaking a word if only you could read the signs and notices that are posted and displayed as directions and advertising. A sign is an immediate communication to him who can read it, and the pronunciation doesn't matter. Here are the messages of some common signs. Some will help you to avoid embarrassment, and others danger. And some of them will merely make life more pleasant.

A DESTRA, To the right
A SINISTRA, To the left
ALT, Stop
ALLARME D'INCENDIO, Fire alarm
APERTO, Open
APPARTAMENTI MOBIGLIATI D'AFFITTARE
 Furnished rooms to let
ASCIUGAMANI, Hand towels

ASPETTATE, Wait
ATTENZIONE, Caution
AVANTI, Go
AVVISO, Warning
CALDO, Warm
CASSIERE, Cashier
CHIESA, Church
CHIUSO, Closed
COLLINA, Hill
CURVA, Curve
CURVA PERICOLOSA, Dangerous curve
DEVIAZIONE, Detour
DIVIETO DI SOSTA, No parking
DONNE, Women
ENTRATA, Entrance
ENTRATA LIBERA, Admission free
È PERICOLOSO, It's dangerous
È PROIBITO PASSARE, No thoroughfare
È VIETATO L'INGRESSO, Keep out
È VIETATO FUMARE, No smoking
FREDDO, Cold
GABINETTO, Lavatory, toilet
INCROCIO FERROVIA, Railroad crossing
INCROCIO PERICOLOSO, Dangerous crossroad
INFORMAZIONI, Information
INGRESSO, Entrance
LAVORI IN CORSO, Men working
LA VIA CHIUSA, No thoroughfare
LIBERO, Free
NON BEVETE L'ACQUA, Do not drink the water
NON ENTRATE, Do not enter
NON GIRATE A DESTRA, No right turn
NON GIRATE A SINISTRA, No left turn

NON TOCCATE, Do not touch
OCCUPATO, Occupied
PEDAGGIO, Toll
PERICOLO, Danger
PONTE STRETTO, Narrow bridge
POSTEGGIO, Parking
PROIBITO, Forbidden
RALLENTARE, Slow, Go slow
RITIRATA, Toilet
SALA D'ASPETTO, Waiting room
SALA DA PRANZO, Dining room
SCUOLA, School
SENSO UNICO, One way
SIGNORE, Women
SIGNORI, Men
SI PERMETTE FUMARE, Smoking allowed
SPINGETE, Push
STANZA DA BAGNO, Bathroom
STRADA STRETTA, Narrow road
SUONATE, Ring
TENETE LA DESTRA, Keep to the right
TIRATE, Pull
UOMINI, Men
USCITA, Exit
VIETATO, Forbidden
VIETATO IL POSTEGGIO, No parking

Numbers, Time and Dates

You may only want to count your change or make an appointment or catch a train, but you will need to know the essentials of counting and telling time if you wish to stay on schedule, buy gifts, or pay for accommodations. In Europe, you should remember, time is told by a twenty-four hour system. Thus 10 P.M. in Italy is 2200 and 10:30 P.M. is 2230.

Cardinal Numbers

one
uno, una, un, un'
oo'-noh, oo'-nah, oon, oon'

two
due
doo'-eh

three
tre
tre

four
quattro
kwaht'-troh

five
cinque
cheen'-kweh

six
sei
seh'-ee

seven
sette
set'-teh

eight
otto
ot'-toh

nine
nove
no'-veh

ten
dieci
dyeh'-chee

eleven
undici
oon'-dee-chee

twelve
dodici
do'-dee-chee

thirteen
tredici
tre'-dee-chee

fourteen
quattordici
kwaht-tor'-dee-chee

fifteen
quindici
kween'-dee-chee

sixteen
sedici
seh'-dee-chee

seventeen
diciassette
dee-chahs-set'-teh

eighteen
diciotto
dee-chot'-toh

nineteen
diciannove
dee-chahn-no'-veh

twenty
venti
ven'-tee

twenty-one
ventuno
ven-too'-noh

twenty-two
ventidue
ven-tee-doo'-eh

thirty
trenta
tren'-tah

thirty·one
trentuno
tren-too'-noh

forty
quaranta
kwah-rahn'-tah

fifty
cinquanta
cheen-kwahn'-tah

sixty
sessanta
ses-sahn'-tah

seventy
settanta
set-tahn'-tah

eighty
ottanta
ot-tahn'-tah

ninety
novanta
no-vahn'-tah

one hundred
cento
chen'-toh

two hundred
duecento
doo-eh-chen'-toh

three hundred
trecento
tre-chen'-toh

five hundred
cinquecento
cheen-kweh-chen'-toh

one thousand
mille
meel'-leh

one million
un milione
oon mee-lyoh'-neh

nineteen hundred seventy- . . .
mille novecento settanta- . . .
meel'-leh no-veh-chen'-toh set-tahn'-tah- . . .

one man
un uomo
oon woh'-moh

one woman
una donna
oo'-nah don'-nah

one child
un bambino (un fanciullo)
oon bahm-bee'-noh (fahn-choool'-loh)

two children
due bambini (fanciulli)
doo'-eh bahm-bee'-nee (fahn-choool'-lee).

two women
due donne
doo'-eh don'-neh

two men
due uomini
doo'-eh woh'-mee-nee

Some Ordinal Numbers

the first
il primo
eel pree'-moh

the second
il secondo
eel seh-kon'-doh

the third
il terzo
eel ter'-tsoh

the fourth
il quarto
eel kwahr'-toh

the fifth
il quinto
eel kween'-toh

the sixth
il sesto
eel ses'-toh

the seventh
il settimo
eel set'-tee-moh

the eighth
l'ottavo
lot-tah'-voh

the ninth
il nono
eel noh'-noh

the tenth
il decimo
eel deh'-chee-moh

the first man
il primo uomo
eel pree'-moh woh'-moh

the first woman
la prima donna
lah pree'-mah don'-nah

the first child
il primo bambino
eel pree'-moh bahm-bee'-noh

the fifth floor
il quinto piano
eel kween'-toh pyah'-noh

the third day
il terzo giorno
eel ter'-tsoh johr'-noh

the fourth street
la quarta strada
lah kwahr'-tah strah'-dah

the second building
il secondo edifizio
*eel seh-kohn'-doh eh-dee-
fee'-tsyoh*

Telling Time

What time is it?
Che ora è?
Keh oh'-rah e?

It's one o'clock.
È l'una.
E loo'-nah.

It's two o'clock.
Sono le due.
Soh'-noh leh doo'-eh.

It's a quarter after two.
Sono le due e un quarto.
*Soh'-noh leh doo'-eh eh
oon kwahr'-toh.*

It's half-past two.
Sono le due e mezza.
Soh'-noh leh doo'-eh eh med'-dzah.

It's a quarter till two.
Sono le due meno un quarto.
Soh'-noh leh doo'-eh meh'-noh oon kwahr'-toh.

It's ten after two.
Sono le due e dieci.
*Soh'-noh leh doo'-eh eh
dyeh'-chee.*

It's ten till two.
Sono le due meno dieci.
*Soh'-noh leh doo'-eh meh'-
noh dyeh'-chee.*

It's five o'clock.
Sono le cinque.
Soh'-noh leh cheen'-kweh.

It's ten o'clock.
Sono le dieci.
Soh'-noh leh dyeh'-chee.

It's noon.
È mezzogiorno.
E med-dzoh-jor'-noh.

It's midnight.
È mezzanotte.
E med-dzah-not'-teh.

It's early.
È presto.
E pre-stoh.

It's late.
È tardi.
E tahr'-dee.

one second
un secondo
oon seh-kon'-doh

five seconds
cinque secondi
cheen'-kweh seh-kon'-dee

one minute
un minuto
oon mee-noo'-toh

five minutes
cinque minuti
cheen'-kweh mee-noo'-tee

one quarter hour
un quarto d'ora
oon kwahr'-toh doh'-rah

one half hour
una mezz'ora
oo'-nah med-dzoh'-rah

one hour
un'ora
oon oh'-rah

five hours
cinque ore
cheen'-kweh oh'-reh

At what time are you leaving?
A che ora parte?
Ah keh oh'-rah pahr'-teh?

When do you arrive?
Quando arriva?
Kwahn'-doh ahr-ree'-vah?

When do you arrive?
Quando arriva?
Kwahn'-doh ahr-ree'-vah?

When will we arrive?
Quando arriveremo?
Kwahn'-doh ahr-ree-veh-reh'-moh?

When shall we meet?
Quando ci incontreremo?
Kwahn'-doh chee een-kon-treh-reh'-moh?

Meet me here at five o'clock.
M'incontri qui alle cinque.
Meen-kon'-tree kwee ahl'-leh cheen'-kweh.

At what time do you get up?
A che ora si alza?
Ah keh oh'-rah see ahl'-tsah?

At what time do you go to bed?
A che ora si corica?
Ah keh oh'-rah see koh'-ree-kah?

Dates

today
oggi
oj'-jee

tomorrow
domani
doh-mah'-nee

yesterday
ieri
ye'-ree

one day
un giorno
oon jor'-noh

two days
due giorni
doo'-eh jor'-nee

five days
cinque giorni
cheen'-kweh jor'-nee

the day after tomorrow
dopo domani
doh'-poh doh-mah'-nee

the day before yesterday
l'altro ieri
lahl'-troh ye'-ree

the morning
la mattina
lah maht-tee'-nah

the afternoon
il pomeriggio
eel poh-me-reej'-joh

the evening
la sera
lah seh'-rah

the night
la notte
lah not'-teh

the week
la settimana
lah set-tee-mah'-nah

the month
il mese
eel meh'-zeh

the year
l'anno
lahn'-noh

last week
la settimana scorsa
lah set-tee-mah'-nah skor'-sah

last month
il mese scorso
eel meh'-zeh skor'-soh

last year
l'anno scorso
lahn'-noh skor'-soh

this week
questa settimana
kwes'-tah set-tee-mah'-nah

this month
questo mese
kwes'-toh meh'-zeh

this year
quest'anno
kwest-ahn'-noh

next week
la settimana ventura (prossima)
lah set-tee-mah'-nah ven-too'-rah (pros'-see-mah)

next month
il mese venturo (prossimo)
*eel meh'-zeh ven-too'-roh
(pros'-see-moh)*

next year
l'anno venturo (prossimo)
*lahn'-noh ven-too'-roh
(pros'-see-moh)*

this morning
stamattina
stah-maht-tee'-nah

yesterday morning
ieri mattina
ye'-ree maht-tee'-nah

tomorrow morning
domani mattina
doh-mah'-nee maht-tee'-nah

this evening
stasera
stah-seh'-rah

yesterday evening
ieri sera
ye'-ree seh'-rah

tomorrow evening
domani sera
doh-mah'-nee seh'-rah

every day
tutti i giorni (ogni giorno)
toot'-tee ee jor'-nee (oh'-nyee jor'-noh)

two days ago
due giorni fa
doo'-eh jor'-nee fah

The Days of the Week

Monday
lunedì
loo-neh-dee'

Tuesday
martedì
mahr-teh-dee'

Wednesday
mercoledì
mer-koh-leh-dee'

Thursday
giovedì
joh-veh-dee'

Friday
venerdì
ve-ner-dee'

Saturday
sabato
sah'-bah-toh

Sunday
domenica
doh-meh'-nee-kah

The Months of the Year

January
gennaio
jen-nah'-yoh

February
febbraio
feb-brah'-yoh

March
marzo
mahr'-tsoh

April
aprile
ah-pree'-leh

May
maggio
mahj'-joh

June
giugno
joo'-nyoh

July
luglio
loo'-lyoh

August
agosto
ah-go'-stoh

September
settembre
set-tem'-breh

October
ottobre
ot-to'-breh

November
novembre
no-vem'-breh

December
dicembre
dee-chem'-breh

The Seasons

the spring
la primavera
lah pree-mah-veh'-rah

the summer
l'estate
le-stah'-teh

the autumn
l'autunno
low-toon'-noh

the winter
l'inverno
leen-ver'-noh

Changing Money

Whether poet or businessman, you will need cash as you travel. Sooner or later every traveler meets the problem of how to manage the exchange. The following phrases cover most situations you will encounter. You will help yourself if you obtain the latest official exchange rate before you leave home, and it can do no harm if you familiarize yourself with the sizes, shapes, and even colors of the various coins and bills. It is wise, too, to take along a small amount of the foreign currency for immediate use on arrival.

Where is the nearest bank?
Dov'è la banca più vicina?
Do-ve' lah bahn'-kah pyoo vee-chee'-nah?

Please write the address.
Scriva l'indirizzo, per piacere
Skree'-vah leen-dee-reet'-tsoh, per pyah-cheh'-reh.

I would like to cash this check.
Vorrei incassare quest'assegno.
Vor-reh'-ee een-kahs-sah'-reh kwest-ahs-seh'-nyoh.

Will you cash this check?
Vuole scontarmi quest'assegno?
Vwoh'-leh skon-tahr'-mee kwest-ahs-seh'-nyoh?

Do you accept travelers' checks?
Accettate assegni di viaggio?
Ahch-chet-tah'-teh ahs-seh'-nyee dee vyahj'-joh?

I want to change some money.
Voglio cambiare del denaro.
Voh'-lyoh kahm-byah'-reh del deh-nah'-roh.

What kind?
Che specie?
Keh speh'-chyeh?

Dollars.	**Pounds.**
Dollari.	Libbre.
Dol'-lah-ree.	*Leeb'-breh.*

What is the rate of exchange for the dollar (pound)?
Qual'è il cambio in dollari (libbre)?
Kwahl-e' eel kahm'-byoh een dol'-lah-ree (leeb'-breh)?

Your passport, please.
Il Suo passaporto, per piacere.
Eel soo'-woh pahs-sah-por'-toh, per pyah-cheh'-reh.

How much do you wish to change?
Quanto desidera cambiare?
Kwahn'-toh deh-zee'-deh-rah kahm-byah'-reh?

I want to change ten dollars.
Voglio cambiare dieci dollari.
Voh'-lyoh kahm-byah'-reh dyah'-chee dol'-lah-ree.

Go to that clerk's window.
Vada allo sportello di quell'impiegato.
Vah'-dah ahl'-loh spor-tel'-loh dee kwel'-leem-pyeh-gah'-toh.

Here's the money.
Ecco il denaro.
Ek'-koh eel deh-nah'-roh.

Please give me some small change.
Per piacere, mi dia della moneta spicciola.
Per pyah-cheh'-reh, mee dee'-yah del'-lah moh-neh'-tah speech'-choh-lah.

Here's your change.
Ecco il resto.
Ek'-koh eel res'-toh.

Please count to see if it's right.
Lo conti, per favore, per vedere se è giusto.
Loh kon'-tee, per fah-voh'-reh, per veh-deh'-reh seh e joos'-toh.

Please sign this receipt.
Firmi questa ricevuta, per piacere.
Feer'-mee kwes'-tah ree-cheh-voo'-tah, per pyah-cheh'-reh.

Can I change money here at the hotel?
Posso cambiare denaro qui in albergo?
Pos'-soh kahm-byah'-reh deh-nah'-roh kwee een ahl-ber'-goh?

I'm expecting some money by mail.
Aspetto denaro per la posta.
Ah-spet'-toh deh-nah'-roh per lah pos'-tah.

Customs

Your first experience with Italian may be with the personnel or fellow passengers on a ship or a plane, but you will really begin to use the language when you come to customs. Here are some phrases that will speed your entry into the country and get you on your way again.

Have you anything to declare?
Ha qualcosa da dichiarare?
Ah kwahl-ko'-zah dah dee-kyah-rah'-reh?

I have nothing to declare.
Non ho niente da dichiarare.
Non oh nyen'-teh dah dee-kyah-rah'-reh.

Your passport, please.
Il passaporto, prego.
Eel pahs-sah-por'-toh, preh'-goh.

Here is my passport.
Ecco il mio passaporto.
Ek'-koh eel mee'-yoh pahs-sah-por'-toh.

Are these your bags?
Sono queste le Sue valige?
Soh'-noh kwes'-teh leh soo'-weh vah-lee'-jeh?

Yes, and here are the keys.
Sì, ed ecco le chiavi.
See, ed ek'-koh leh kyah'-vee.

Open this box.
Apra questa scatola.
Ah'-prah kwes'-tah skah'-toh-lah.

Close your bags.
Chiuda le valige.
Kyoo'-dah leh vah-lee'-jeh.

Have you any cigarettes or tobacco?
Ha delle sigarette o tabacco?
Ah del'-leh see-gah-ret'-teh oh tah-bahk'-koh?

I have only some cigarettes.
Ho soltanto qualche sigaretta.
Oh sol-tahn'-toh kwahl'-keh see-gah-ret'-teh.

You must pay duty.
Lei deve pagare dazio.
Leh'-ee deh'-veh pah-gah'-reh dah'-tsyoh.

They are for my personal use.
Sono per il mio uso personale.
Soh'-noh per eel mee'-yoh oo'-zoh per-soh-nah'-leh.

How much must I pay?
Quanto devo pagare?
Kwahn'-toh deh'-voh pah-gah'-reh?

You must pay . . .
Deve pagare . . .
Deh'-veh pah-gah'-reh . . .

May I go now?
Posso andare adesso?
Pos'-soh ahn-dah'-reh ah-dehs'-soh?

Is that all?
Questo è tutto?
Kwes'-toh e toot'-toh?

Porter, please carry this luggage.
Facchino, per piacere, porti questo bagaglio.
Fahk-kee'-noh, per pyah-cheh'-reh por'-tee kwes'-toh bah-gahl'-yoh.

At the Hotel

Your accommodations may be a deluxe hotel, a modest hotel, a pension, or whatever, but it is important to be able to express your needs to be sure you get what you want. Outside of the cities, of course, few people are likely to be able to help you if you do not speak Italian, so we have given you the most useful expressions to cover most situations. They may make the difference between getting the room you want and having to settle for something less.

Which is the best hotel?
Qual'è il miglior albergo?
Kwahl-e' eel meel-yohr' ahl-ber'-goh?

This is a good hotel.
Questo è un buon albergo.
Kwes'-toh e oon bwon ahl-ber'-goh.

I like this hotel.
Mi piace quest'albergo.
Mee pyah'-cheh kwest-ahl-ber'-goh.

3 Pensions

I would like to have a room here.
Vorrei prendere una camera qui.
Vor-reh'-ee pren'-de-reh oo'-nah kah'-meh-rah kwee.

A single room.
Una camera a un letto.
*Oo'-nah kah'-meh-rah ah
   oon let'-toh.*

A double room.
Una camera a due letti.
*Oo'-nah kah'-meh-rah ah
   doo'-eh let'-tee.*

A room with (without) bath.
Una camera con (senza) bagno.
Oo'-nah kah'-meh-rah kon (sehn'-tsah) bah'-nyoh.

May I see the room?
Posso vedere la camera?
*Pos'-soh veh-deh'-reh lah
   kah'-meh-rah?*

Is there a shower?
C'è una doccia?
Che oo'-nah doch'-chah?

This is a large room.
Questa è una camera grande.
Kwes'-tah e oo'-nah kah'-meh-rah grahn'-deh.

This room is too small.
Questa camera è troppo piccola.
Kwes'-tah kah'-meh-rah e trop'-poh peek'-koh-lah.

The room faces the street.
La camera dà sulla strada.
Lah kah'-meh-rah dah sool'-lah strah'-dah.

Do you have a quieter room?
Ha una camera più silenziosa?
Ah oo'-nah kah'-meh-rah pyoo see-len-tsyoh'-zah?

— due gente. Que costa. Rimanremo tre notтеs. Arrivaremo a las sietа or ocho

Do you have a room with a view of the ocean (court)?
Ha una camera con vista sull'oceano (sul cortile)?
*Ah oo'-nah kah'-meh-rah kon vees'-tah sool-loh-cheh'-
   ah-noh (sool kor-tee'-leh)?*

What is the price of this room?
Qual'è il prezzo di questa camera?
Kwahl-e' eel preht'-tsoh dee kwes'-tah kah'-meh-rah?

That's much too expensive.   **That's very good.**
È troppo cara.   È molto buono.
E trop'-poh kah'-rah.   *E mol'-toh bwoh'-noh.*

Does the price include breakfast?
È compresa la prima colazione nel prezzo?
*Eh kom-preh'-zah lah pree'-mah koh-lah-tsyoh'-neh nel
    pret'-tsoh?*

Do you have a restaurant in the hotel?
C'è un ristorante nell'albergo?
Cheh oon rees-toh-rahn'-teh nel-lahl-ber'-goh?

Must we eat our meals in the hotel restaurant?
Dobbiamo mangiare i pasti nel ristorante dell'albergo?
*Dob-byah'-moh mahn-jah'-reh ee pahs'-tee nel rees-toh-
    rahn'-teh del-lahl-ber'-goh?*

Where is the dining room?
Dov'è la sala da pranzo?
Do-ve' lah sah'-lah dah prahn'-dzoh?

We will stay here.
Rimarremo qui.
Ree-mahr-reh'-moh kwee.

How long will you stay?
Quanto tempo rimarrà?
Kwahn'-toh tem'-poh ree-mahr-rah'?

I will stay three weeks.
Rimarrò tre settimane.
Ree-mahr-roh'-tre set-tee-mah'-neh.

We will stay three weeks.
Rimarremo tre settimane.
Ree-mahr-reh'-moh tre set-tee-mah'-neh.

Please fill out this card.
Riempia questa carta, per favore.
Ree-em-pee'-yah kwes'-tah kahr'-tah, per fah-voh'-reh.

My key, please.
La mia chiave, prego.
Lah mee'-yah kyah'-veh, preh'-goh.

What number, sir?
Che numero, signore?
Keh noo'-me-roh, see-nyoh'-reh?

I have lost my key.
Ho perduto la mia chiave.
Oh per-doo'-toh lah mee'-yah kyah'-veh.

Where is the elevator?
Dov'è l'ascensore?
Do-ve' lah-shen-soh'-reh?

Where is the key to my room?
Dov'è la chiave della mia camera?
Do-ve' lah kyah'-veh del'-lah mee-yah kah'-meh-rah?

Take my suitcase to my room.
Porti la mia valigia alla mia camera.
Por'-tee lah mee'-yah vah-lee'-jah ahl'-lah mee'-yah kah'-meh-rah.

Where is the bathroom?
Dov'è la stanza da bagno?
Do-ve' lah stahn'-tsah dah bah'-nyoh?

Open the window, please.
Apra la finestra, per favore.
Ah'-prah lah fee-nes'-trah, per fah'-voh'-reh.

Close the window, please.
Chiuda la finestra, per favore.
Kyoo'-dah lah fee-nes'-trah, per fah-voh'-reh.

Please call the chambermaid.
Chiami la cameriera, per favore.
Kyah'-mee lah kah-meh-ree-ye'-rah, per fah-voh'-reh.

I want to have these shirts washed.
Desidero far lavare queste camice.
Deh-zee'-de-roh fahr lah-vah'-reh kwes'-teh kah-mee'-cheh.

This is not my handkerchief.
Questo non è il mio fazzoletto.
Kwes'-toh non e eel mee'-yoh faht-tsoh-let'-toh.

I want a towel and some soap.
Desidero un asciugamano e del sapone.
Deh-zee'-de-roh oon ah-shoo-gah-mah'-noh eh del sah-poh'-neh.

I want a clean towel.
Voglio un asciugamano pulito.
Vohl'-yoh oon ah-shoo-gah-mah'-noh poo-lee'-toh.

Please wake me at seven o'clock.
Per favore, mi svegli alle sette.
Per fah-voh'-reh, mee zve'-lyee ahl'-leh set'-teh.

We are leaving tomorrow.
Partiamo domani.
Pahr-tyah'-moh doh-mah'-nee.

Take my luggage down.
Faccia scendere il mio bagaglio.
Fahch'-chah shen'-de-reh eel mee'-yoh bah-gahl'-yoh.

Are there any letters for me?
Ci sono delle lettere per me?
Chee soh'-noh del'-leh let'-te-reh per meh?

I need some postage stamps.
Ho bisogno di alcuni francobolli.
Oh bee-zoh'-nyoh dee ahl-koo'-nee frahn-koh-bol'-lee.

Using the Telephone

Many visitors to foreign lands avoid using the telephone when they should not. Of course, gesturing and pointing are of no avail when you cannot see the person to whom you are speaking and have to depend entirely on what you hear and say. Still, it is possible to communicate if you make an effort. If there is difficulty, remember to ask the other person to speak slowly. It's your best assurance that the message will get through.

Where is there a telephone?
Dove c'è un telefono?
Do'-veh che oon te-le'-foh-noh?

I would like to telephone.
Vorrei telefonare.
Vor-reh'-ee te-le-foh-nah'-reh.

I would like to make a (long-distance) call to . . .
Vorrei fare una telefonata (interurbana) a . . .
Vor-reh'-ee fah'-reh oo'-nah te-le-foh-nah'-tah (een-ter-oor-bah'-nah) ah . .

What is the telephone number?
Qual'è il numero telefonico?
Kwahl-e' eel noo'-me-roh te-le-foh'-nee-koh?

Where is the telephone book?
Dov'è l'elenco telefonico?
Do-ve' leh-lehn'-koh te-le-foh'-nee-koh?

My number is . . .
Il mio numero è . . .
Eel mee'-yoh noo'-me-roh eh . . .

Operator!
Telefonista!
Te-le-foh-nees'-tah!

I want number . . .
Desidero il numero . . .
Deh-zee'-de-roh eel noo'-me-roh . . .

Can I dial this number?
Posso fare questo numero?
Pos'-soh fah'-reh kwes'-toh noo'-me-roh?

How much is a telephone call to . . . ?
Quanto costa una chiamata telefonica a . . . ?
Kwahn'-toh kos'-tah oo'-nah kyah-mah'-tah te-le-foh'-nee-kah ah . . . ?

I am ringing.
Sto suonando.
Stoh swoh-nahn'-doh.

Please do not hang up.
Un momento, per favore.
Oon moh-men'-toh, per fah-voh'-reh.

Deposit coins.
Depositi della moneta.
Deh-poh'-zee-tee del'-lah moh-neh'-tah.

They do not answer.
Non rispondono.
Non ree-spon'-doh-noh.

Please dial again.
Faccia il numero di nuovo, per piacere.
Fahch'-chah eel noo'-me-roh dee nwoh'-voh, per pyah-cheh'-reh.

The line is busy.
La linea è occupata.
Lah lee'-neh-yah e ok-koo-pah'-tah.

Who is speaking?
Chi parla?
Kee pahr'-lah?

May I speak to . . . ?
Posso parlare con . . . ?
Pos'-soh pahr-lah'-reh kon . . . ?

He (she) is not in.
Non c'è.
Non che.

Please speak more slowly.
Parli più lentamente (adagio), per favore.
Pahr'-lee pyoo len-tah-men'-teh (ah-dah'-joh), per fah-voh'-reh.

Getting Around by Taxi and Bus

The drivers of taxis and buses almost never speak English, which may be fortunate when you relish a few peaceful moments. However, you will have to tell them where you're going, or want to go, and for that we've provided some handy phrases.

Call a taxi, please.
Chiami un tassì, per piacere.
Kyah'-mee oon tahs-see', per pyah-cheh'-reh.

Put my luggage into the taxi.
Metta il mio bagaglio nel tassì.
Met'-tah eel mee'-yoh bah-gahl'-yoh nel tahs-see'.

Driver, are you free?
Autista, è libero?
Ow'-tees'-tah, e lee'-be-roh?

Where do you wish to go?
Dove desidera andare?
Do'-veh deh-zee'-de-rah ahn-dah'-reh?

Drive to the railroad station (airport).
Mi conduca alla stazione ferroviaria (all'aeroporto).
Meek on-doo'-kah ahl'-lah stah-tsyoh'-neh fer-roh-vee'-yah-ree-yah (ahll-ah-eh-roh-por'-toh).

How much is the ride from here to the hotel?
Quanto costa la passeggiata da qui all'albergo?
Kwahn'-toh kos'-tah lah pahs-sehj-jah'-tah dah kwee ahl-ahl-ber'-goh?

Stop here!
Fermi qui!
Fer'-mee kwee!

I want to get out here.
Voglio scendere qui.
Vohl'-yoh shen'-de-reh kwee.

Wait until I come back.
Aspetti finchè torni.
Ahs-pet'-tee feen-keh' tor'-nee.

Wait for me here.
Mi aspetti qui.
Mee ahs-pet'-tee kwee.

Drive a little farther.
Vada un po' più avanti.
Vah'-dah oon po pyoo ah-vahn'-tee.

Please drive carefully.
Vada con cura, per favore.
Vah'-dah kon koo'-rah, per fah-voh'-reh.

Please drive slowly.
Vada adagio, per favore.
Vah'-dah ah-dah'-joh, per fah-voh'-reh.

Turn to the left (right) here.
Giri a sinistra (destra) qui.
Jee'-ree ah see-nees'-trah (des'-trah) kwee.

Drive straight ahead.
Vada sempre diritto.
Vah'-dah sem'-preh dee-reet'-toh.

How much is the fare?
Quanto è la tariffa?
Kwahn'-toh e lah tah-reef'-fah?

Which bus goes downtown?
Quale autobus va al centro della città?
Kwah'-leh ow-toh-boos' vah ahl chen'-troh del'-lah cheet-tah'?

Bus number . . .
L'autobus numero . . .
Low-toh-boos' noo'-me-roh . . .

Does the bus stop here?
L'autobus si ferma qui?
Low-toh-boos' see fer'-mah kwee?

Which bus goes to . . . ?
Quale autobus va a . . . ?
Kwah'-leh ow-toh-boos' vah ah . . . ?

Get on the bus here.
Salga nell'autobus qui.
Sahl'-gah nell-ow-toh-boos' kwee.

Get off the bus here.
Scenda dall'autobus qui.
Shen'-dah dahll-ow-toh-boos' kwee.

Please tell me when we arrive at . . . street.
Mi dica, per piacere, quando arriveremo alla via . . .
Mee dee'-kah per pyah-cheh'-reh kwahn'-doh ahr-ree-ve-reh'-moh ahl'-lah vee'-yah . . .

Does this bus go to the museum?
Va quest'autobus al museo?
Vah kwest-ow-toh-boos' ahl moo-zeh'-oh?

Where must I transfer?
Dove devo trasferire?
Do'-veh deh'-voh trahs-fe-ree'-reh?

When does the last bus leave?
Quando parte l'ultimo autobus?
Kwahn'-doh pahr'-teh lool'-tee-moh ow-toh-boos'?

Eating and Drinking

Merely going abroad is thrill enough for some persons; for others the high points are likely to be the hours spent at the table. Getting to know and appreciate the national cuisine and learning how to order native dishes are extra thrills for many travelers. Here, to the phrases that are necessary to order your meals, we have added a menu reader of the most typical dishes of the cuisine in the countries where Italian is spoken.

I'm hungry.	**I'm thirsty.**
Ho fame.	Ho sete.
Oh fah'-meh.	*Oh seh'-teh.*
Are you hungry?	**Are you thirsty?**
Ha fame?	Ha sete?
Ah fah'-meh?	*Ah seh'-teh?*

I'm not hungry.
Non ho fame.
Non oh fah'-meh.

I'm not thirsty.
Non ho sete.
Non oh seh'-teh.

Do you want to eat now?
Vuole mangiare adesso?
Vwoh'-leh mahn-jah'-reh ah-dehs'-soh?

Let's eat now.
Mangiamo adesso.
Mahn-jah'-moh ah-dehs'-soh.

Where is there a good restaurant?
Dove c'è un buon ristorante?
Do'-veh che oon bwon ree-stoh-rahn'-teh?

The meals.
I pasti.
Ee pahs'-tee.

breakfast
la prima colazione
lah pree'-mah koh-lah-tsyoh'-neh

lunch
la seconda colazione
lah seh-kon'-dah koh-lah-tsyoh'-neh

dinner
il pranzo
eel prahn'-dzoh

supper
la cena
lah cheh'-nah

At what time is breakfast (lunch, dinner)?
A che ora si serve la prima colazione (la seconda colazione, il pranzo)?
Ah keh oh'-rah see ser'-veh lah pree'-mah koh-lah-tsyoh'-neh (lah seh-kon'-dah koh-lah-tsyoh'-neh, eel prahn'-dzoh)?

I want breakfast in my room.
Desidero la prima colazione nella mia camera.
Deh-zee'-deh-roh lah pree'-mah koh-lah-tsyoh'-neh nel'-lah mee'-yah kah'-mee-rah.

I would like . . .
Vorrei . . .
Vor-reh'-ee . . .

---

eggs
uova
woh'-vah

fried eggs
uova fritte, uova alpiatto
woh'-vah freet'-teh, woh'-vah ahl pyaht'-toh

scrambled eggs
uova strapazzate
woh'-vah strah-pahd-dzah'-teh

two soft-boiled eggs
due uova bollite
doo'-eh woh'-vah bol-lee'-teh

a poached egg
un uovo affogato
oon woh'-voh ahf-foh-gah'-toh

bacon
pancetta, lardo
pahn-chet'-tah, lahr'-doh

bread and butter
pane e burro
pah'-neh eh boor'-roh

black coffee
caffè nero
kahf-fe' neh'-roh

coffee with milk
caffè latte
kahf-fe' laht'-teh

coffee without milk
caffè senza latte
kahf-fe' sehn'-tsah laht'-teh

milk
il latte
el laht'-teh

tea
il tè
eel te

ham
prosciutto
proh-shoot'-toh

cold meat
carne fredda
kahr'-neh frehd'-dah

rolls
panini
pah-nee'-nee

Breakfast is ready.
La prima colazione è servita.
Lah pree'-mah koh-lah-
tsyoh'-neh e ser-vee'-tah.

Dinner is being served.
Il pranzo è servito.
Eel prahn'-dzoh e ser-vee'-
toh.

A table for two, please.
Una tavola per due, per favore.
Oo'-nah tah'-voh-lah per doo'-eh, per fah-voh'-reh.

Where is the waitress?
Dov'è la cameriera?
Do-ve' lah kah-me-ree-yeh'-rah?

Waiter (waitress), the menu, please.
Cameriere (cameriera), la lista, per favore.
Kah-me-ree-yeh'-reh (kah-me-ree-yeh'-rah), lah lees'-tah,
per fah-voh'-reh.

Waiter, please bring an ashtray.
Cameriere, porti un portacenere, per favore.
Kah-me-ree-yeh'-reh, por'-tee oon por-tah-cheh'-neh-reh,
per fah-voh'-reh.

What do you recommend?
Che raccomanda? / Che mi consiglia?
Keh rahk-koh-mahn'-dah? / Keh mee kon-seel'-yah?

Do you recommend . . . ?
Raccomanda . . . ? / Mi consiglia . . . ?
Rahk-koh-mahn'-dah . . . ? / Mee kon-seel'-yah . . . ?

Bring me some coffee now, please.
Mi porti un po' di caffè adesso, per favore.
Mee por'-tee oon po dee kahf-fe' ah-dehs'-soh, per fah-voh'-
reh.

More butter, please.
Più burro, per favore.
Pyoo boor'-roh, per fah-voh'-reh.

Bring some more sugar.
Porti più zucchero.
Por'-tee pyoo dzook'-ke-roh.

Bring me a glass of water, please.
Mi porti un bicchiere d'acqua, per favore.
Mee por'-tee oon beek-kee-ye'-reh dahk'-kwah, per fah-voh'-reh.

This coffee is cold.
Questo caffè è freddo.
Kwes'-toh kahf-fe' e frehd'-doh.

Do you take milk and sugar?
Prende latte e zucchero?
Pren'-deh laht'-teh eh dzook'-ke-roh?

The Condiments

the salt
il sale
eel sah'-leh

the pepper
il pepe
eel peh'-peh

the sugar
lo zucchero
loh dzook'-ke-roh

the oil
l'olio
loh'-lyoh

the vinegar
l'aceto
lah-cheh'-toh

the mustard
il senape, la mostarda
eel seh'-nah-peh, lah mos-tãhr'-dah

No sugar, thank you.
Niente zucchero, grazie.
Nyen'-teh dzook'-ke-roh, grah'-tsee-yeh.

We eat only fruit for breakfast.
Mangiamo solo frutta alla prima colazione.
Mahn-jah'-moh soh'-loh froot'-tah ahl'-lah pree'-mah koh-lah-tsyoh'-neh.

This butter is not fresh.
Questo burro non è fresco.
Kwes'-toh boor'-roh non e fres'-koh.

This milk is warm.
Questo latte è caldo.
Kwes'-toh laht'-teh e kahl'-doh.

This milk is sour.
Questo latte è acido.
Kwes'-toh laht'-teh e ah'-chee-doh.

I would like a glass of cold milk.
Vorrei un bicchiere di latte freddo.
Vor-reh'-ee oon beek-kee-ye'-reh dee laht'-teh frehd'-doh.

Foods and Beverages

the fish
il pesce
eel peh'-sheh

fruit
la frutta
lah froot'-tah

the meat
la carne
lah kahr'-neh

the water
l'acqua
lahk'-kwah

vegetables
i legumi
ee leh-goo'-mee

the beer
la birra
lah beer'-rah

the wine
il vino
eel vee'-noh

the bread
il pane
eel pah'-neh

Another cup of coffee?
Un'altra tazza di caffè?
Oon ahl'-trah taht'-tsah dee kahf-fe'?

Another cup of tea?
Un'altra tazza di tè?
Oon ahl'-trah taht'-tsah dee te?

Do you want some more tea?
Vuole più tè?
Vwoh'-leh pyoo te?

Nothing more, thank you.
Nient'altro, grazie.
Nyent-ahl'-troh, grah'-tsee-yeh.

At what time are the meals in this hotel?
A che ora si servono i pasti in quest'albergo?
Ah keh oh'-rah see ser'-voh-noh ee pahs'-tee een kwest-ahl-ber'-goh?

We dine at seven o'clock.
Pranziamo alle sette.
Prahn-dzyah'-moh ahl'-leh set'-teh.

---

the cheese
il formaggio
eel for-mahj'-joh

the milk
il latte
eel laht'-teh

the butter
il burro
eel boor'-roh

the honey
il miele
eel myeh'-leh

the jam
la confettura
lah kon-fet-too'-rah

the salad
l'insalata
leen-sah-lah'-tah

the soup
la zuppa, la minestra
lah dzoop'-pah, lah mee-nes'-trah

Here they dine at eight o'clock.
Qui mangiano alle otto.
Kwee mahn'-jah-noh ahl'-leh ot'-toh.

Please reserve a table for us.
Prenoti una tavola per noi, per piacere.
Preh-noh'-tee oo'-nah tah'-voh-lah per noy, per pyah-cheh'-reh.

Do you want soup?
Vuole zuppa?
Vwoh'-leh dzoop'-pah?

The Setting

a spoon
un cucchiaio
oon kook-kee-ah'-ee-yoh

a knife
un coltello
oon kol-tel'-loh

a fork
una forchetta
oo'-nah for-ket'-tah

a plate
un piatto
oon pyaht'-toh

a napkin
un tovagliolo
oon toh-vahl-yoh'-loh

a small spoon
un cucchiaino
oon kook-kee-ah-ee'-noh

a small knife
un coltello piccolo
oon kol-tel'-loh peek'-koh-loh

a small fork
una forchetta piccola
oo'-nah for-ket'-tah peek'-koh-lah

a tray
un vassoio
oon vahs-soh'-yoh

Bring me a fork (a knife, a spoon).
Mi porti una forchetta (un coltello, un cucchiaio).
Mee por'-tee oo'-nah for-ket'-tah (oon kol-tel'-loh, oon kook-kee-ah'-ee-yoh).

This fork is dirty.
Questa forchetta è sporca.
Kwes'-tah for-ket'-tah e spor'-kah.

This spoon isn't clean.
Questo cucchiaio non è pulito.
Kwes'-toh kook-kee-ah'-ee-yoh non e poo-lee'-toh.

Please bring me a napkin.
Mi porti un tovagliolo, per favore.
Mee por'-tee oon toh-vahl-yoh'-loh, per fah-voh'-reh.

I would like a glass of wine.
Vorrei un bicchiere di vino.
Vor-reh'-ee oon beek-kee-ye'-reh dee vee'-noh.

A glass of red (white) wine.
Un bicchiere di vino rosso (bianco).
Oon beek-kee-ye'-reh dee vee'-noh ros'-soh (byahn'-koh).

A bottle of wine.
Una bottiglia di vino.
Oo'-nah bot-teel'-yah dee vee'-noh.

This wine is too warm.
Questo vino è troppo caldo.
Kwes'-toh vee'-noh e trop'-poh kahl'-doh.

A half-bottle.
Una mezza bottiglia.
Oo'-nah med'-dzah bot-teel'-yah.

Please bring some ice.
Porti un po' di ghiaccio, per favore.
Por'-tee oon po dee gyahch'-choh, per fah-voh'-reh.

I didn't order this.
Non ho ordinato questo.
Non oh or-dee-nah'-toh kwes'-toh.

A glass of beer.
Un bicchiere di birra.
Oon beek-kee-ye'-reh dee beer'-rah.

A bottle of beer.
Una bottiglia di birra.
Oo'-nah bot-teel'-yah dee beer'-rah.

To your health!
Alla Sua (Vostra) salute!
Ahl'-lah Soo'-wah (Vos'-trah) sah-loo'-teh!

Enjoy your meal!
Buon appetito!
Bwon ahp-peh-tee'-toh!

This tablecloth is not clean.
Questa tovaglia non è pulita.
Kwes'-tah toh-vahl'-yah non e poo-lee'-tah.

Do you eat fish?
Mangia pesce?
Mahn'-jah peh'-sheh?

He doesn't eat meat.
Lui non mangia carne.
Loo'-ee non mahn'-jah kahr'-neh.

I don't eat dessert.
Io non mangio dolci.
Ee'-yoh non mahn'-joh dohl'-chee.

He would like some ice cream.
Vorrebbe gelato.
Vor-reb'-beh jeh-lah'-toh.

Waiter, the check, please.
Cameriere, il conto, per favore.
Kah-me-ree-yeh'-reh, eel kon'-toh, per fah-voh'-reh.

How much do I owe you?
Quento Le devo?
Kwahn'-toh Leh deh'-voh?

Is the tip included?
È compreso il servizio?
E kom-preh-zoh eel ser-vee'-tsee-yoh?

Where do I pay?
Dove pago?
Do'-veh pah'-goh?

At the cashier's booth.
Alla cassa.
Ahl'-lah kahs'-sah.

I have already paid.
Ho già pagato.
Oh jah pah-gah'-toh.

Here is a tip.
Ecco una mancia.
Ek'-koh oo'-nah mahn'-chah.

I left the tip on the table.
Ho lasciato la mancia sulla tavola.
Oh lah-shah'-toh lah mahn'-chah sool'-lah tah'-voh-lah.

There is a mistake in the bill.
C'è uno sbaglio nel conto.
Che oo'-noh zbahl'-yoh nel kon'-toh.

Menu
Reader

Zuppe ed Antipasti Soups and Appetizers

Antipasto (*ahn-tee-pahs'-toh*) Hor d'oeuvres.

Brodo (*broh'-doh*) Consomme.

Minestrone (*mee-nes-troh'-neh*) Vegetable soup with various regional additions.

Pastina in brodo (*pahs-tee'-nah een broh'-doh*) Pasta in soup broth.

Zuppa alla pavese (*dzoop'-pah ahl'-lah pah-veh'-zeh*) Egg soup.

Zuppa di pesce (*dzoop'-pah dee peh'-sheh*) Fish soup.

Farinacei Pasta Dishes

Cannelloni (*kahn-nel-loh'-nee*) Meat-filled pasta, baked in cheese and tomato sauce.

Ravioli alla fiorentina (*rah-vyoh'-lee ahl'-lah fyoh-ren-tee'-* ...) Cheese ravioli.

    alla vegetariana (*ahl'-lah veh-jeh-tah-ree-yah'-nah*) Ravioli with tomato sauce.

    fatti in casa (*faht-tee een kah-zah*) Home-made ravioli.

Spaghetti alla Bolognese (*spah-get'-tee ahl'-lah boh-lohn-yeh'-zeh*) Spaghetti with meat sauce.

    alla bosaiola (*ahl'-lah boh-zah-yoh'-lah*) Spaghetti with tuna, mushrooms and cheese.

    alla carbonara (*ahl'-lah kahr-boh-nah'-rah*) Spaghetti cooked in egg and bacon.

    al pomodoro (*ahl poh-moh-doh'-roh*) Spaghetti with tomato sauce.

    al sugo di carne (*ahl soo'-goh dee kahr'-neh*) Spaghetti with meat sauce.

    alle vongole (*ahl-leh von-goh-leh*) Spaghetti with clam sauce.

Taglierini, fettuccine (*tahl-yeh-ree'-nee, fet-tooch-chee'-neh*) Noodles.

Pesce Fish

Acciughe (*ahch-choo'-geh*) Anchovies.

Aragosta (*ah-rah-gos'-tah*) Lobster.

Filetto di sogliola (*fee-let'-toh dee sohl'-yoh-lah*) Filet of sole.

Fritto misto (*freet'-toh mees'-toh*) Assorted tiny fried fish. Italian specialty.

Gamberi (*gahm'-beh-ree*) Shrimps.

Ostriche (*os'-tree-keh*) Oysters.

Sgombro (*zgom'-broh*) Mackerel.

Tonno (*ton'-noh*) Tuna fish.

Trotta (*trot'-tah*) Trout.

Carne Meat

Bistecca (*bees-tek'-kah*) Steak.

    all'inglese (*ahl-leen-gleh'-zeh*) Rare.

    ben cotta (*ben kot'-tah*) Well done.

Cervello (*cher-vel'-loh*) Brains.

Cotoletta alla bolognese (*koh-toh-let'-tah ahl'-lah boh-lohn-yeh'-zeh*) Veal cutlet with melted cheese.
    alla Milanese (*ahl'-lah mee-lah-neh'-zeh*) Breaded veal cutlet
Fegato (*feh'-gah-toh*) Liver.
Maiale (*mah-yah'-leh*) Pork.
Manzo lesso (*mahn'-dzoh les'-soh*) Boiled beef.
Pancetta (*pahn-chet'-tah*) Bacon.
Pollo alla cacciatora (*pol'-loh ahl'-lah kahch-chah-toh'-rah*) Stewed chicken.
    alla diavolo (*ahl'-lah dyah'-voh-loh*) Chicken broiled with herbs.
Prosciutto (*proh-shoot'-toh*) Thinly sliced, dark spicy ham.
Rosbif (*roz-beef'*) Roast beef.
Salsicce (*sahl-seech'-cheh*) Sausages.
Saltimbocca (*sahl-teem-bok'-kah*) Veal and ham dish. Italian specialty.
Spezzatino di manzo (*spet-tsah-tee'-noh dee mahn'-dzoh*) Beef stew.
Vitello al forno (*vee-tel'-loh ahl for'-noh*) Roast veal.

Verdura ed Insalata Vegetables and Salads

Asparagi (*ahs-pah'-rah-jee*) Asparagus.
Carciofi (*kahr-choh'-fee*) Artichokes.
Cavolo (*kah'-voh-loh*) Cabbage.
Cetrioli (*cheh-tree-yoh'-lee*) Cucumbers.
Cipolle (*chee-pol'-leh*) Onions.
Fagiolini (*fah-joh-lee'-nee*) String beans.
Finocchio (*fee-nok'-kyoh*) Type of celery.
Funghi (*foon'-gee*) Mushrooms.
Insalata mista (*een-sah-lah'-tah mees'-tah*) Mixed salad.
Insalata verde (*een-sah-lah'-tah ver'-deh*) Lettuce salad.
Lattuga (*laht-too'-gah*) Lettuce.
Melanzana (*meh-lahn-dzah'-nah*) Eggplant.
Olive (*oh-lee'-veh*) Olives.
Peperoni (*peh-peh-roh'-nee*) Green peppers.

Pomodori (*poh-moh-doh'-ree*) Tomatoes.
Spinaci (*spee-nah'-chee*) Spinach.
Zucchini (*dzook-kee'-nee*) Summer squash.

Frutte e Dolci Fruits and Desserts

Ananasso (*ah-nah-nahs'-soh*) Pineapple.
Arance (*ah-rahn'-cheh*) Oranges.
Banane (*bah-nah'-neh*) Bananas.
Cassata (*kahs-sah'-tah*) Ice cream with fruit.
Ciliegie (*chee-lee-yeh'-jeh*) Cherries.
Composta di frutta (*kom-pos'-tah dee froot'-tah*) Stewed fruit.
Formaggio (*for-mahj'-joh*) Cheese.
Gelato (*jeh-lah'-toh*) Ice cream.
Mela (*meh'-lah*) Apple.
Pasticceria (*pahs-teech-cheh-ree'-yah*) Pastry.
Pesca alla melba (*pes'-kah ahl'-lah mel'-bah*) Peach melba.
Pere (*peh'-reh*) Pears.
Pompelmo (*pom-pel'-moh*) Grapefruit.
Torta (*tor'-tah*) Cake.
Uva (*oo'-vah*) Grapes.

Bibite Beverages

Acqua (*ahk'-kwah*) Water.
Aranciata (*ah-rahn-chah'-tah*) Orangeade.
Birra (*beer'-rah*) Beer.
Caffè (*kahf-feh'*) Coffee.
 caffè latte (*kahf-feh' laht'-teh*) Coffee with milk.
Latte (*laht'-teh*) Milk.
Limonata (*lee-moh-nah'-tah*) Lemonade.
Sherry dolce (*sher'-ree dol'-cheh*) Sweet sherry.
Sherry secco (*sher'-ree sek'-koh*) Dry sherry.
Succhi di frutta (*sook'-kee dee froot'-tah*) Fruit juices.
Tè (*teh*) Tea.
Vino bianco (*vee'-noh byahn'-koh*) White wine.
Vino rosso (*vee'-noh ros'-soh*) Red wine.

Shopping

Shopping abroad is always an adventure and frequently a
delight. It's not only the varied merchandise that you may
buy to take home as gifts, but the sheer pleasure of making
yourself understood. It's important to know, and to be
able to explain, exactly what it is that you want since,
obviously, you won't be able to trot downtown a week
later to make an exchange. You'll discover, too, that sizes
and weights are different; so we have included conversion
tables here. Here are the typical questions that you or the
salesman might ask or the statements you may make
during your shopping trips.

I would like to go shopping.
Vorrei fare delle compre.
Vor-reh'-ee fah'-reh del'-leh kom'-preh.

At what time do the stores open?
A che ora si aprono i negozi?
Ah keh oh'-rah see ah'-proh-noh ee neh-goh'-tsee?

At what time do the stores close?
A che ora si chiudono i negozi?
Ah keh oh'-rah see kyoo'-doh-noh ee neh-goh'-tsee?

Where is there . . . ?
Dove c'è . . . ?
Do'-veh che . . . ?

---

an antique shop.
un negozio di antichità.
oon neh-goh'-tsyoh dee ahn-tee-kee-tah'.

a book store.
una libreria.
oo'-nah lee-bre-ree'-yah.

a candy store.
una confetteria.
oo'-nah kon-fet-te-ree'-yah.

a department store.
un grande magazzino.
oon grahn'-deh mah-gahd-dzee'-noh.

a dressmaker.
una sarta.
oo'-nah sahr'-tah.

a druggist.
un droghiere.
oon droh-gyeh'-reh.

a drugstore.
una farmacia.
oo'-nah fahr-mah-chee'-yah.

a florist.
un fioraio.
oon fee-yoh-rah'-yoh.

a grocery.
una bottega di comestibili.
oo'-nah bot-teh'-gah dee ko-mes-tee'-bee-lee.

a greengrocer.
un verduraio.
oon ver-doo-rah'-yoh.

May I help you?
Posso servirLe?
Pos'-soh ser-veer'-leh?

Will you help me, please?
Per piacere, mi aiuterà?
*Per pyah-cheh'-reh, mee
ah-yoo-te-rah'?*

Are you being served? (m)
È stato servito?
Eh stah'-toh ser-vee'-toh?

Are you being served? (f)
È stata servita?
E stah'-tah ser-vee'-tah?

What do you wish?
Che cosa desidera?
Keh ko'-zah deh-zee'-deh-rah?

---

a hat shop.
una cappelleria.
*oo'-nah kahp-pel-le-ree'-
yah.*

a jewelry store.
una gioielleria.
oo'-nah joy-el-le-ree'-yah.

a perfumery.
una profumeria.
*oo'-nah proh-fee-me-ree'-
yah.*

a photography shop.
un negozio di fotografia.
*oon neh-goh'-tsyoh dee
foh-toh-grah-fee'-yah.*

a shoe store.
una calzoleria.
*oo'-nah kahl-tsoh-le-ree'-
yah.*

a tailor.
un sarto.
oon sahr'-toh.

a tobacconist.
una tabaccaio.
*oo'-nah tah-bahk-kah'-
yoh.*

a toy store.
un negozio di giocattoli.
*oon neh-goh'-tsyoh dee
joh-kaht'-toh-lee.*

a watchmaker.
un orologiaio.
oon oh-roh-loh-jah'-yoh.

I would like . . .
Vorrei . . .
Vor-reh'-ee . . .

a brassiere.
un reggipetto.
oon rej-jee-pet'-toh.

a handkerchief.
un fazzoletto.
oon faht-tshoh-let'-toh.

panties.
mutandine.
moo-tahn-dee'-neh.

shoes.
scarpe.
skahr'-peh.

a skirt.
una gonna.
oo'-nah gon'-nah.

socks.
calzette.
kahl-tset'-teh.

a suit.
un abito.
oon ah'-bee-toh.

a tie.
una cravatta.
oo'-nah krah-vaht'-tah.

underwear.
biancheria.
byahn-ke-ree'-yah.

gloves.
dei guanti.
deh'-ee gwahn'-tee.

a hat.
un cappello.
oon kahp-pel'-loh.

a shirt.
una camicia.
oo'-nah kah-mee'-chah.

shorts.
mutande.
moo-tahn'-deh.

a slip.
una sottana.
oo'-nah sot-tah'-nah.

stockings.
calze.
kahl'-tseh.

a sweater.
un maglione.
oon mah-lyoh'-neh.

an undershirt.
una camiciola.
oo'-nah kah-mee'-choh-lah.

I would like to buy . . .
Vorrei comprare . . .
Vor-reh'-ee kom-prah'-reh . . .

a battery.
una batteria.
oo'-nah baht-te-ree'-yah.

a camera.
una macchina fotografica.
*oo'-nah mahk'-kee-nah
foh-toh-grah'-fee-kah.*

film.
pellicola, film.
pel-lee'-koh-lah, feelm.

flashbulbs.
lampadine fotografiche.
*lahm-pah-dee'-neh foh-
toh-grah'-fee-keh.*

a pen.
una penna.
oo'-nah pen'-nah.

a pencil.
una matita.
oo'-nah mah-tee'-tah.

postcards.
cartoline postali.
*kahr-toh-lee'-neh pos-
tah'-lee.*

stamps.
francobolli.
frahn-koh-bol'-lee.

lotion.
lozione.
loh-tsyoh'-neh.

powder.
cipria.
cheep'-ree-yah.

razor blades.
lame da rasoio.
*lah'-meh dah rah-zoh'-
yoh.*

shampoo.
shampoo, frizionamento.
*shahm-poo', free-tsyoh-
nah-men'-toh.*

shaving cream.
crema da barba.
kreh'-mah dah bahr'-bah.

soap.
sapone.
sah-poh'-neh.

toothbrush.
spazzolino da denti.
*spaht-tshoh-lee'-noh dah
den'-tee.*

toothpaste.
pasta dentifricia.
*pahs'-tah den-tee-free'-
chah.*

Do you sell . . . ?
Vendete . . . ?
Ven-deh'-teh . . . ?

Do you have . . . ?
Ci avete . . . ?
Chee ah-veh'-teh . . . ?

Please show me some . . .
Per piacere, mi mostri . . .
Per pyah-cheh'-reh, mee mos'-tree . . .

What size, please?
Che misura, per favore?
Keh mee-zoo'-rah, per fah-voh'-reh?

Try on these . . .
Provi questi . . .
Proh'-vee kwes'-tee . . .

How much does it cost?
Quanto costa?
Kwahn'-toh kos'-tah?

How much do they cost?
Quanto costano?
Kwahn'-toh kos'-tah-noh?

That is too expensive.
Questo è troppo caro.
Kwes'-toh e trop'-poh kah'-roh.

That is cheap.
Questo è a buon mercato.
Ques'-toh e ah bwon mer-kah'-toh.

I like this one.
Questo mi piace.
Kwes'-toh mee pyah'-cheh.

I will take this one.
Prenderò questo.
Pren-de-roh' kwes'-toh.

---

cigar.
sigaro.
see'-gah-roh.

cigarettes.
sigarette.
see-gah-ret'-teh.

flint.
pietra focaia.
pye'-trah foh-kah'-yah.

fluid.
benzina.
ben-dzee'-nah.

lighter.
accendi-sigari.
ahch-cheh'-dee-see'-gah-ree.

matches.
fiammiferi.
fee-yahm-mee'-fe-ree.

I don't like this color.
Questo colore non mi piace.
Kwes'-toh koh-loh'-reh non mee pyah'-cheh.

I prefer it in . . .
Lo preferisco in . . .
Loh preh-fe-rees'-koh een . . .

---

black	**blue**	**brown**	**gray**
nero	azzurro	bruno, marrone	grigio
neh'-roh	*ahd-dzoor'-roh*	*broo'-noh, mahr'-roh'-neh*	*gree'-joh*
green	**red**	**white**	**yellow**
verde	rosso	bianco	giallo
ver'-deh	*ros'-soh*	*byahn'-koh*	*jahl'-loh*
dark		**light**	
scuro		chiaro	
skoo'-roh		*kyah'-roh*	

Sale
Vendita
Ven'-dee-tah

For Sale
Da vendere
Dah ven'-deh-reh

Clearance Sale
Vendita a stralcio, svendita
Ven'-dee-tah ah strahl'-choh, sven'-dee-tah

This dress is too short.
Questo vestito è troppo corto.
Kwes'-toh ves-tee'-toh e trop'-poh kor'-toh.

This skirt is too long.
Questa gonna è troppo lunga.
Kwes'-tah gon'-nah e trop'-poh loon'-gah.

I would like to see a white shirt.
Vorrei vedere una camicia bianca.
Vor-reh'-ee veh-deh'-reh oo'-nah kah-mee'-chah byan'-kah.

He would like to see some white shirts.
Lui vorrebbe vedere alcune camice bianche.
Loo'-ee vor-reb'-beh veh-deh'-reh ahl-koo'-neh kah-mee'-cheh byan'-keh.

The sleeves are too wide.
Le maniche sono troppo larghe.
Leh mah'-nee-keh soh'-noh trop'-poh lahr'-geh.

The sleeves are too narrow.
Le maniche sono troppo strette.
Leh mah'-nee-keh soh'-noh trop'-poh stret'-teh.

I would like to see some shoes.
Vorrei vedere delle scarpe.
Vor-reh'-ee veh-deh'-reh del'-leh skahr'-peh.

A pair of black (brown) shoes.
Un paio di scarpe nere (marroni).
Oon pah'-yoh dee skahr'-peh neh'-reh (mahr-roh'-nee).

Try this pair on.
Provi questo paio.
Proh'-vee kwes'-toh pah'-yoh.

They are too narrow.
Sono troppo strette.
Soh'-noh trop'-poh stret'-teh.

They are too (tight, loose, long, short).
Sono troppo (strette, sciolte, lunghe, corte).
Soh'-noh trop'-poh (stret'-teh, shol'-teh, loon'-geh, kor'-teh).

They are not big enough.
Non sono abbastanza grandi.
Non soh'-noh ahb-bahs-tahn'-tsah grahn'-dee.

Do you sell cigarettes?
Vendete sigarette?
Ven-deh'-teh see-gah-ret'-teh?

Do you have matches?
Avete fiammiferi?
Ah-veh'-teh fee-yahm-mee'-fe-ree?

I want to buy needles, pins, and some thread.
Voglio comprare aghi, spilli e del filo.
Vohl'-yoh kom-prah'-reh ah'-gee, speel'-lee eh del fee'-loh.

How many do you want?
Quanti ne vuole?
Kwahn'-tee neh vwoh'-leh?

Anything else?
Qualche altra cosa?
Kwahl'-keh ahl'-trah ko'-zah?

No, thank you. That's all.
No, grazie. Questo è tutto.
Noh, grah'-tsee-yeh. Kwes'-toh e toot'-toh.

I'll take it (them) with me.
Lo (Li) prenderò con me.
Loh (lee) pren-de-roh' kon meh.

Will you wrap it, please?
Vuole avvolgerlo, per favore?
Vwoh'-leh ahv-vol'-jer-loh, per fah-voh'-reh?

Send it to the hotel.
Lo mandi in albergo.
Loh mahn'-dee een ahl-ber'-goh.

Pack it (them) for shipment to . . .
Lo (Li) impacchi per spedizione a . . .
Loh (lee) eem-pahk'-kee per speh-dee-tsyoh'-neh ah . . .

Here is the bill.
Ecco la fattura.
Ek'-koh lah faht-too'-rah.

Is there a discount?
C'è uno sconto?
Cheh oo'-noh skon'-toh?

I will pay cash.
Pagherò in denaro contante.
Pah-ge-roh' een deh-nah'-roh kon-tahn'-teh.

CLOTHING SIZE CONVERSIONS: *Women*

Dresses, Suits and Coats

American:	8	10	12	14	16	18
British:	30	32	34	36	38	40
Continental:	36	38	40	42	44	46

Blouses and Sweaters

American:	32	34	36	38	40	42	44
British:	34	36	38	40	42	44	46
Continental:	40	42	44	46	48	50	52

Stockings

American & British:	8	8½	9	9½	10	10½	11
Continental:	35	36	37	38	39	40	41

Shoes

American:	5	5½	6	6½	7	7½	8	8½	9
British:	3½	4	4½	5	5½	6	6½	7	7½
Continental:	35	35	36	37	38	38	38½	39	40

Gloves

American, British and Continental sizes are the same.

CLOTHING SIZE CONVERSIONS: *Men*

Suits, Sweaters and Overcoats

American & British:	34	36	38	40	42	44	46	48
Continental:	44	46	48	50	52	54	56	58

Shirts

American & British:	14	14½	15	15½	16	16½	17	17½
Continental:	36	37	38	39	40	41	42	43

Socks

American and British:	9½	10	10½	11	11½	12	12½
Continental:	39	40	41	42	43	44	45

Shoes

American:	7	7½	8	8½	9	9½	10	10½	11	11½
British:	6½	7	7½	8	8½	9	9½	10	10½	11
Continental:	39	40	41	42	43	43	44	44	45	45

Getting Around by Automobile

Since few attendants who work at garages and stations speak English, some ability in Italian will be very useful. Your car will need gasoline, of course, and probably some regular servicing. And should there be some problem with it, a lot of time and energy will be saved if you can explain your needs.

I would like to hire a car.
Vorrei noleggiare una macchina.
Vor-reh'-ee noh-lej-jah'-reh oo'-nah mahk'-kee-nah.

How much does a car cost per day?
Quanto costa una macchina al giorno?
Kwahn'-toh kos'-tah oo'-nah mahk'-kee-nah ahl jor'-noh?

How much per kilometer?
Quanto per chilometro?
Kwahn'-toh per kee-loh'-meh-troh?

Is gasoline expensive in this country?
È cara la benzina in questo paese?
E kah'-rah lah ben-dzee'-nah een kwes'-toh pah-eh'-zeh?

Is there a deposit?
C'è un deposito?
Cheh oon deh-poh'-zee-toh?

I would like a car with seatbelts and an outside mirror, please.
Vorrei una macchina còn cinture di posto e uno specchio esteriore, per favore.
Vor-reł.'-ee oo'-nah mahk'-kee-nah kon cheen-too'-reh dee pos'-toh eh oo'-noh spek'-kyoh es-te-ree-yoh'-reh, per fah-voh'-reh.

I will (will not) take the car out of the country.
Prenderò (Non prenderò) la macchina fuori del paese.
Pren-deh-roh' (non pren-deh-roh') lah mahk'-kee-nah fwoh'-ree del pah-eh'-zeh.

I want to leave it in . . .
Voglio lasciarla a . . .
Vohl'-yoh lah-shahr'-lah ah . . .

How much is the insurance per day?
Quanto è l'assicurazione al giorno?
Kwahn'-toh eh las-see-koo-rah-tsyoh'-neh ahl jor'-noh?

Here is the registration and the key.
Ecco la registrazione e la chiave.
Ek'-koh lah reh-jees-trah-tsyoh'-neh eh lah kyah'-veh.

Where is there a gas station?
Dove c'è una pompa di benzina?
Do'-veh che oo'-nah pom'-pah dee ben-dzee'-nah?

a garage?
un'autorimessa, un garage?
oon ow-toh-ree-mes'-sah, oon gah-rah'-jeh?

Fill it up.
Lo riempia.
Loh ree-em-pee'-yah.

Premium.
Superiore.
Soo-peh-ree-yoh'-reh.

Regular.
Ordinario.
Ord-dee-nah'-ree-yoh.

I want twenty liters of gasoline.
Voglio venti litri di benzina.
Vohl'-yoh ven'-tee lee'-tree dee ben-dzee'-nah.

I also need some oil.
Anche mi occorre un po' d'olio.
Ahn'-keh mee ok-kor'-reh oon po doh'-lyoh.

Please put in some water.
Metta dentro un po' d'acqua, per favore.
Met'-tah den'-troh oon po dahk'-kwah, per fah-voh'-reh.

Wash the car, please.
Lavi la macchina, per piacere.
Lah'-vee lah mahk'-kee-nah, per pyah-cheh'-reh.

Please inspect the tires.
Esamini le gomme (i pneumatici), per favore.
Eh-zah-mee'-nee leh gom'-meh (ee pneh-oo-mah'-tee-chee), per fah-voh'-reh.

Put in some air.
Metta dentro un po' d'aria.
Met'-tah den'-troh oon po dah'-ree-yah.

Is there a mechanic here?
C'è un meccanico qui?
Che oon mek-kah'-nee-koh kwee?

Can you fix a flat tire?
Può riparare una gomma forata?
Pwoh ree-pah-rah'-reh oo'-nah gom'-mah foh-rah'-tah?

How long will it take?
Quanto tempo ci vorrà?
Kwahn'-toh tem'-poh chee vor-rah'?

Have you a road map?
Ha una carta stradale?
Ah oo'-nah kahr'-tah strah-dah'-leh?

Where does this road go to?
Dove va questa strada?
Do'-veh vah kwes'-tah strah'-dah?

Is this the road to . . . ?
È questa la strada per . . . ?
E kwes'-tah lah strah'-dah per . . ?

Is the road good?
È buona la strada?
E bwoh'-nah lah strah'-dah?

A narrow road.
Una strada stretta.
Oo'-nah strah'-dah stret'-tah.

A wide road.
Una strada larga.
Oo'-nah strah'-dah lahr'-gah.

A narrow bridge.
un ponte stretto.
Oon pon'-teh stret'-toh.

A bad road.
Una cattiva strada.
Oo'-nah kaht-tee'-vah strah'-dah.

This road is slippery when it's wet.
Questa strada è scivolosa quando è bagnata.
Kwes'-tah strah'-dah e shee-voh-loh'-zah kwahn'-doh e bah-nyah'-tah.

Is there a speed limit here?
C'è un limite di velocità qui?
Che oon lee'-mee-teh dee veh-loh-chee-tah' kwee?

You were driving too fast.
Lei conduceva troppo veloce.
Leh'-ee kon-doo-cheh'-vah trop'-poh veh-loh'-cheh.

You must pay the fine.
Lei deve pagare la multa.
Leh'-ee deh'-veh pah-gah'-reh lah mool'-tah.

May I leave the car here?
Posso lasciare la macchina qui?
Pos'-soh lah-sha'-reh lah mahk'-kee-nah kwee?

May I park here?
Posso parcheggiare qui?
Pos'-soh pahr-kehj-jah'-reh kwee?

Where is the nearest garage?
Dov'è l'autorimessa più vicina?
Do-ve' low-toh-ree-mes'-sah pyoo vee-chee'-nah?

This car isn't running well.
Questa macchina non va bene.
Kwes'-tah mahk-kee'-nah non vah beh'-neh.

I have a driver's license.
Ho un patente.
Oh oon pah-ten'-teh.

Please check . . .
Per piacere, esamini . . .
Per pyah-cheh'-reh eh-zah-mee'-nee . . .

Can you fix it?
Può ripararlo?
Pwoh ree-pah-rahr'-loh?

How long will it take?
Quanto tempo ci vorrà?
Kwahn'-toh tem'-poh chee vor-rah'?

Your car is ready.
La Sua macchina è pronta.
Lah Soo'-wah mahk'-kee-nah e pron'-tah.

Drive carefully!
Conduca con cura!
Kon-doo'-kah kon koo'-rah!

Please wipe the windshield.
Per piacere, pulisca la parabrezza.
Per pyah-cheh'-reh, poo-lees'-kah lah pah-rah-bret'-tsah.

I don't know what the matter is.
Non so ciò che c'è.
Non soh choh keh che.

I think it's . . .	**Is it . . . ?**
Credo che è	È . . . ?
Creh'-doh keh e . . .	*E . . . ?*

the accelerator.	**the air filter.**
l'acceleratore.	il filtro d'aria.
lahch-cheh-leh-rah-toh'-reh.	*eel feel'-troh dah'-ree-yah.*
the battery.	**the brakes.**
la batteria.	i freni.
lah baht-teh-ree'-yah.	*ee freh'-nee.*
the carburetor.	**the clutch.**
il carburatore.	la frizione.
eel kahr-boo-rah-toh'-reh.	*lah free-tsyoh'-neh.*
the lights.	**the motor.**
i fari.	il motore.
ee fah'-ree.	*eel moh-toh'-reh.*
the spark plugs.	**the tires.**
le candele.	le gomme, i pneumatici.
leh kahn-deh'-leh.	*leh gom'-meh, ee pneh-oo-mah'-tee-chee.*
the wheel.	**the wheels.**
la ruota.	le ruote.
lah rwoh'-tah.	*leh rwoh'-teh.*
the front wheel.	**the back wheel.**
la ruota anteriore.	la ruota posteriore.
lah rwoh'-tah ahn-te-ree-yoh'-reh.	*lah rwoh'-tah pos-te-ree-yoh'-reh.*

Priority road ahead

Some International Road Signs

 = RED

 = BLUE

 = BLACK

Stop

Dangerous curve

Right curve

Double curve

Intersection

Intersection with secondary road

Railroad crossing
with gates

Railroad crossing
without gates

Road work

Pedestrian
crossing

Children

Road narrows

Uneven road

Slippery road

Traffic circle
ahead

Danger

Closed to
all vehicles

No entry

No left turn

No U turn

Overtaking
prohibited

Speed limit

Customs

No parking

Direction to
be followed

Traffic circle

No parking

Getting Around by Train

The railroad is the most frequently used means of transportation by travelers abroad. Schedules and timetables are usually readily understandable — if they are available and visible — but otherwise, in arranging your travel by train, you will need to use some of these phrases.

The railroad station.
La stazione ferroviaria.
Lah stah-tsyoh'-neh fer-roh-vee-yah'-ree-yah.

The train.
Il treno.
Eel treh'-noh.

Drive to the railroad station.
Mi conduca alla stazione ferroviaria.
Mee kon-doo'-kah ahl'-lah stah-tsyoh'-neh fer-roh-vee-yah'-ree-yah.

I need a porter.
Mi occorre un facchino.
Mee ok-kor'-reh oon fahk-kee'-noh.

Is this my cabin?
È questa la mia cabina?
E kwes'-tah lah mee'-yah kah-bee'-nah?

Steward, do you have the key to my cabin?
Cameriere, ha la chiave della mia cabina?
*Kah-meh-ree-ye'-reh, ah lah kyah'-veh del'-lah mee'-yah
    kah-bee'-nah?*

I'm looking for the dining room.
Cerco la sala da pranzo.
Cher'-koh lah sah'-lah dah prahn'-dzoh.

We want a table for two.
Vogliamo una tavola per due.
Vohl-yah'-moh oo'-nah tah'-voh-lah per doo'-eh.

A first-class cabin.
Una cabina di prima classe.
Oo'-nah kah-bee'-nah dee pree'-mah klahs'-seh.

A second-class cabin.
Una cabina di seconda classe.
Oo'-nah kah-bee'-nah dee seh-kon'-dah klahs'-seh.

Let's go on deck.   **I would like a deck chair.**
Andiamo sul ponte.   Vorrei una sedia a sdraio.
Ahn-dyah'-moh sool pon'-   *Vor-reh'-ee oo'-nah seh'-*
teh.   *dyah ah zdrah'-yoh.*

I would like to eat by the swimming pool.
Vorrei mangiare vicino alla piscina.
*Vor-reh'-ee mahn-jah'-reh vee-chee'-noh ahl'-lah pee-shee'-
    nah.*

The ship arrives at seven o'clock.
La nave arriva alle sette.
Lah nah'-veh ahr-ree'-vah ahl'-leh set'-teh.

When do we go ashore?
Quando scendiamo a terra?
Kwahn'-doh shen-dyah'-moh ah ter'-rah?

Where is the gangplank?
Dov'è la passerella (lo scalandrone)?
Do-ve' lah pahs-se-rel'-lah (loh skah-lahn-droh'-neh)?

The landing card, please.
Il permesso (cartoncino) di sbarco, prego.
*Eel per-mes'-soh (kahr-ton-chee'-noh) dee zbahr'-koh,
preh'-goh.*

I wasn't seasick at all!
Non avevo mal di mare affatto!
Non ah-veh'-voh mahl dee mah'-reh ahf-faht'-toh!

Have a good trip!
Buon viaggio!
Bwon vyahj'-joh!

I want to go to the airport.
Voglio andare all'aeroporto.
Vohl'-yoh ahn-dah'-reh ahll-ah-eh-roh-por'-toh.

Drive me to the airport.
Mi conduca all'aeroporto.
Mee kon-doo'-kah ahll-ah-eh-roh-por'-toh.

When does the plane leave? | **When does it arrive?**
Quando parte l'aeroplano? | Quando arriva?
Kwahn'-doh pahr'-teh lah- | *Kwahn'-doh ahr-ree'-vah?*
eh-roh-plah'-noh?

Flight number . . . leaves at . . .
Il volo numero . . . parte alle . . .
Eel voh'-loh noo'-me-roh . . . pahr'-teh ahl'-leh . . .

From which gate?
Da che porta?
Dah keh por'-tah?

I want to reconfirm my flight.
Voglio riconfirmare il mio volo.
Vohl'-yoh ree-kon-feer-mah'-reh eel mee'-yoh voh'-loh.

Ticket, please.
Il biglietto, prego.
Eel bee-lyet'-toh, preh'-goh.

Boarding pass, please.
Il permesso d'imbarco, prego.
Eel per-mes'-soh deem-bahr'-koh, preh'-goh.

Please fasten your seat belts.
Attaccate le cinture, prego.
Aht-tahk-kah'-teh leh cheen-too'-reh, preh'-goh.

No smoking.
Vietato fumare.
Vyeh-tah'-toh foo-mah'-reh.

Stewardess, a small pillow, please.
Hostess, un guanciale piccolo, per piacere.
*Ohs-tess, oon gwahn-chah'-leh peek'-koh-loh, per pyah-
    cheh'-reh.*

I fly to Europe every year.
Io volo all'Europa ogni anno.
Ee'-yoh voh'-loh ahll-eh-oo-roh'-pah oh'-nyee ahn'-noh.

The airplane is taking off!
L'aeroplano decolla.
Lah-eh-roh-plah'-noh deh-kol'-lah.

Is a meal served during this flight?
Si serve un pasto durante questo volo?
See ser'-veh oon pahs'-toh doo-rahn'-teh kwes'-toh voh'-loh?

The airplane will land in ten minutes.
L'aeroplano atterrerà fra dieci minuti.
Lah-eh-roh-plah'-noh aht-ter-re-rah' frah dyeh'-chee mee-noo'-tee.

There will be a delay.
Ci sarà un ritardo.
Chee sah-rah' oon ree-tahr'-doh.

There's the runway!
Ecco la pista!
Ek'-koh lah pees'-tah!

We have arrived.
Siamo arrivati.
Syah'-moh ahr-ree-vah'-tee.

Health

We hope you will never need the phrases you will find in
this section; but emergencies do arise, and sickness does
overwhelm. Since a physician's diagnosis often depends
on what you, the patient, can tell him, you will want to
make your woes clearly understood. If you have a chronic
medical problem, you will want to have prescriptions or
medical descriptions of the difficulty in hand or translated
before you leave on your trip.

I need a doctor.
Ho bisogno d'un medico.
Oh bee-zoh'-nyoh doon meh'-dee-koh.

Send for a doctor.
Faccia venire un medico.
Fahch'-chah veh-nee'-reh oon meh'-dee-koh.

Send for a doctor.
Mandi chiamare un medico.
Mahn'-dee kyah-mah'-reh oon meh'-dee-koh.

Are you the doctor?
È Lei il medico?
E leh'-ee eel meh'-dee-koh?

What is the matter with you?
Che cosa ha?
Keh ko'-zah ah?

I don't feel well.
Non mi sento bene.
Non mee sen'-toh beh'-neh.

I am sick.
Sono ammalato (*f*) / ammalata (*f*).
Soh'-noh ahm-mah-lah'-toh (m) / -tah (f).

How long have you been sick?
Da quanto tempo è ammalato?
Dah kwahn'-toh tem'-poh e ahm-mah-lah'-toh?

I have a headache.
Ho mal di testa.
Oh mahl dee tes'-tah.

Where is the hospital?
Dov'è l'ospedale?
Do-ve' los-peh-dah'-leh?

Is there a drugstore near here?
C'è una farmacia qui vicino?
Che oo'-nah fahr-mah-chee'-yah kwee vee-chee'-noh?

I have a stomach ache.
Ho mal di stomaco.
Oh mahl dee stoh'-mah-koh.

Where does it hurt?
Dove Le duole?
Do'-veh leh dwoh'-leh?

My leg hurts.
La gamba mi fa male.
Lah gahm'-bah mee fah mah'-leh.

Do I have a fever?
Ho una febbre?
Oh oo'-nah feb'-breh?

My finger is bleeding.
Il mio dito sanguina.
Eel mee'-yoh dee'-toh sahn'-gwee-nah.

---

the arm, the arms
il braccio, le braccia
eel brahch'-choh, leh brahch-chah.

the back
la schiena
lah skyeh'-nah

the bladder
la vescica
lah veh-shee'-kah

the bone
l'osso
los'-soh

the chest
il petto
eel pet'-toh

the ear, the ears
l'orecchio, gli orecchi
loh-rek'-kyoh, lyee oh-rek'-kee.

the elbow
il gomito
eel goh'-mee-toh

the eye, the eyes
l'occhio, gli occhi
lok'-kyoh, lyee ok'-kee

the face
il viso, la faccia
eel vee'-zoh, lah fahch'-chah

the finger
il dito
eel dee'-toh

the foot, the feet
il piede, i piedi
eel pyeh'-deh, ee pyeh'-dee

the forehead
la fronte
lah fron'-teh

I have burned myself.
Mi sono bruciato (*m*) / bruciata (*f*).
Mee soh'-noh broo-chah'-toh (m) / -tah (f).

You must stay in bed.
Deve stare a letto.
Deh'-veh stah'-reh ah let'-toh.

How long?
Quanto tempo?
Kwahn'-toh tem'-poh?

---

the hair
i capelli
ee kah-pel'-lee

my hair
i miei capelli
ee myeh'-ee kah-pel'-lee

the hand, the hands
la mano, le mani
lah mah'-noh, leh mah'-nee

the head
la testa
lah tes'-tah

the heart
il cuore
eel kwoh'-reh

the hip
l'anca
lahn'-kah

the joint
la giuntura
lah joon-too'-rah

the kidneys
i reni
ee reh'-nee

the knee
il ginocchio
eel jee-nok'-kyoh

the leg, the legs
la gamba, le gambe
lah gahm'-bah, leh gahm'-beh

the liver
il fegato
eel feh'-gah-toh

the lung, the lungs
il polmone, i polmoni
eel pol-moh'-neh, ee pol-moh'-nee

At least two days.
Al meno due giorni.
Ahl meh'-noh doo'-eh jor'-nee.

Show me your tongue.
Mi mostri la lingua.
Mee mos'-tree lah leen'-gwah.

---

the mouth
la bocca
lah bok'-kah

the muscle
il muscolo
eel moos'-koh-loh

the neck
il collo
eel kol'-loh

the nose
il naso
eel nah'-zoh

the shoulder
la spalla
lah spahl'-lah

the skin
la pelle
lah pel'-leh

the skull
il cranio
eel krah'-nyoh

the spine
la spina dorsale
lah spee'-nah dor-sah'-leh

the stomach
lo stomaco
loh stoh'-mah-koh

the thigh
la coscia
lah ko'-shah

the throat
la gola
lah goh'-lah

the thumb
il pollice
eel pol'-lee-cheh

the toe
il dito del piede
eel dee'-toh del pyeh'-deh

the tooth, the teeth
il dente, i denti
eel den'-teh, ee den'-tee

the waist
la vita
lah vee'-tah

the wrist
il polso
eel pol'-soh

Lie down.
Si corichi.
See koh'-ree-kee.

Get up.
Si alzi.
See ahl'-tsee.

I have a cold.
Sono raffreddato (*m*) / raffreddata (*f*).
Soh'-noh rahf-frehd-dah'-toh (m) / -tah (f).

Do you smoke?
Fuma?
Foo'-mah?

Yes, I smoke.
Sì, fumo.
See, foo'-moh.

No, I don't smoke.
No, non fumo.
Noh, non foo'-moh.

Do you sleep well?
Dorme bene?
Dor'-meh beh'-neh?

No, I don't sleep well.
No, non dormo bene.
Noh, non dor'-moh beh'-neh.

I cough frequently.
Tossisco spesso.
Tos-sees'-koh spehs'-soh.

Take this medicine three times a day.
Prenda questa medicina tre volte al giorno.
Pren'-dah kwes'-tah meh-dee-chee'-nah tre vol'-teh ahl jor'-noh.

Here is a prescription.
Ecco una prescrizione.
Ek'-koh oo'-nah preh-skree-tsyoh'-neh.

Can you come again tomorrow?
Può venire di nuovo domani?
Pwoh veh-nee'-reh dee nwoh'-voh doh-mah'-nee?

Yes, I can come.
Sì, posso venire.
See, pos'-soh veh-nee'-reh.

I will come later.
Verrò più tardi.
Ver-roh' pyoo tahr'-dee.

He's a good doctor.
Lui è un buon medico.
*Loo'-ee e oon bwon meh'-
dee-koh.*

Sightseeing

No phrase book can possibly supply you with all the phrases you might want in the infinite number of situations, emotions, likes, and dislikes you will encounter in your travels. The basics are here, but they can only be a beginning. The dictionary at the back of this book will supply you with a larger vocabulary to use with the phrases given here. In addition, local bilingual or multilingual guides are usually very helpful in supplying other language information concerning a given situation. If an unusual phrase is required, ask him and it will be given to you gladly.

I would like to go sightseeing.
Vorrei girare per vedere delle curiosità.
Vor-reh'-ee jee-rah'-reh per veh-deh'-reh del'-leh koo-ree-yoh-zee-tah'.

How long does the tour last?
Quanto tempo dura il giro?
Kwahn'-toh tem-poh doo'-rah eel jee'-roh?

It lasts three hours.
Dura tre ore.
Doo'-rah tre oh'-reh.

Are you the guide?
È Lei la guida?
E leh'-ee lah gwee'-dah?

What is the name of this place?
Come si chiama questo luogo?
Ko'-meh see kyah'-mah kwes'-toh lwoh'-goh?

Are the museums open today?
Sono aperti i musei oggi?
Soh'-noh ah-per'-tee ee moo-zeh'-ee oj'-jee?

No, the museums are closed today.
No, i musei sono chiusi oggi.
Noh, ee moo-zeh'-ee soh'-noh kyoo'-zee oj'-jee.

The stores are open.
I negozi sono aperti.
Ee neh-goh'-tsee soh'-noh ah-per'-tee.

I would like to visit an art museum.
Vorrei visitare un museo d'arte.
Vor-reh'-ee vee-zee-tah'-reh oon moo-zeh'-oh dahr'-teh.

Is there an exhibition there now?
C'è un' esposizione lì adesso?
Che oon es-poh-zee-tsyoh'-neh lee ah-des'-soh?

I would like to see the city.
Vorrei vedere la città.
Vor-reh'-ee veh-deh'-reh lah cheet-tah'.

What is the name of that church?
Come si chiama quella chiesa?
Ko'-meh see kyah'-mah kwel'-lah kyeh'-zah?

May we go in?
Possiamo entrare?
Pos-syah'-moh en-trah'-reh?

Is the old church closed this morning?
È chiusa la vecchia chiesa stamattina?
E kyoo'-zah lah vek'-kyah kyeh'-zah stah-maht-tee'-nah?

Will it be open this evening?
Sarà aperta stasera?
Sah-rah' ah-per'-tah stah-seh'-rah?

This is the main square of the city.
Questa è la piazza principale della città.
*Kwes'-tah e lah pyaht'-tsah preen-chee-pah'-leh del'-lah
   cheet-tah'.*

May I take pictures here?
Posso fare delle fotografie qui?
Pos'-soh fah'-reh del'-leh fot-toh-grah-fee'-yeh kwee?

We have walked a lot.
Abbiamo camminato molto.
Ahb-byah'-moh kahm-mee-nah'-toh mol'-toh.

I am tired.	**Let's sit down.**
Sono stanco (*m*) / stanca (*f*).	Sediamoci.
Soh'-noh stahn'-koh (m) /	*Seh-dyah'-moh-chee.*
-kah (f).	

Where does this street lead to?
Dove va questa strada?
Do'-veh vah kwes'-tah strah'-dah?

To the cathedral.
Alla cattedrale.
Ahl'-lah kaht-teh-drah'-leh.

What is that monument?
Qual'è quel monumento?
Kwahl-e' kwel moh-noo-men'-toh?

Is that a theater?
È quello un teatro?
E kwel'-loh oon teh-yah'-troh?

It's a movie house.
È un cinema.
E oon chee'-neh-mah.

What is the name of this park?
Come si chiama questo parco?
Ko'-meh see kyah'-mah kwes'-toh pahr'-koh?

We cross the street here.
Attraversiamo la strada qui.
Aht-trah-ver-syah'-moh lah strah'-dah kwee.

Will we visit a castle?
Visiteremo un castello?
Vee-zee-teh-reh'-moh oon kahs-tel'-loh?

We will visit a palace.
Visiteremo un palazzo.
Vee-zee-teh-reh'-moh oon pah-laht'-tsoh.

Who lives in this palace?
Chi abita questo palazzo?
Kee ah'-bee-tah kwes'-toh pah-laht'-tsoh?

Nobody lives here.
Nessuno abita qui.
Nes-soo'-noh ah'-bee-tah kwee.

What is the name of this river?
Come si chiama questo fiume?
Ko'-meh see kyah'-mah kwes'-toh fyoo'-meh?

This is the longest bridge in the city.
Questo è il ponte più lungo della città.
Kwes'-toh e eel pon'-teh pyoo loon'-goh del'-lah cheet-tah'.

There's too much water in the boat.
C'è tropp'acqua nella barca.
Che trop-pahk'-kwah nel'-lah bahr'-kah.

Is our hotel near the river?
È il nostro albergo vicino al fiume?
E eel nos'-troh ahl-ber'-goh vee-chee'-noh ahl fyoo'-meh?

This is the shopping center.
Questo è il centro di compre.
Kwes'-toh e eel chen'-troh dee kom'-preh.

Is it far from here to the beach?
È lontano da qui alla spiaggia?
E lon-tah'-noh dah kwee ahl'-lah spyahj'-jah?

I would like to go swimming this morning.
Vorrei andare a fare il bagno stamattina.
Vor-reh'-ee ahn-dah'-reh ah fah'-reh eel bah'-nyoh stah-maht-tee'-nah.

If it doesn't rain, we'll go there.
Se no piove, ci andremo.
Seh non pyo'-veh, chee ahn-dreh'-moh.

Thank you for an interesting tour.
Grazie per un giro interessante.
Grah'-tsee-yeh per oon jee'-roh een-te-res-sahn'-teh.

Thank you very much for it.
La ringrazio molto.
Lah reen-grah'-tsyoh mol'-toh.

I like it.	**I liked it.**
Mi piace.	Mi è piaciuto.
Mee pyah'-cheh.	*Mee e pyah-choo'-toh.*

DICTIONARY

Some Tips On Italian Grammar

Gender Nouns in Italian are either masculine or feminine. This is important to know since the form of other parts of speech (articles, adjectives, pronouns) depends on whether they modify or appear in connection with a masculine or feminine noun. The indefinite and definite articles and adjectives, always agree with the noun in number and gender.

As a rule, nouns ending in "o" are masculine and those ending in "a" are feminine. Nouns ending in "e" in the singular may be either masculine or feminine, and the correct gender must be learned when the word is first encountered.

The definite articles (*the*) are *il* for the masculine singular nouns beginning with a single consonant (except "z") or with two consonants (except "s" plus consonant), and *lo* for masculine singular nouns beginning with "z" or with "s" plus consonant. The definite article *l'* is used before masculine and feminine singular nouns beginning with a vowel. The definite article *la* is used before feminine singular nouns beginning with a consonant or consonants. In plural nouns, *i* replaces the article *il*, and *gli* replaces *lo* and *l'* with masculins nouns. *Le* replaces *la* and *l'* with feminine noune. Notice the following:

il fiume (the river)	i fiumi (the rivers)
il vestito (the dress)	i vestiti (the dresses)
l'uomo (the man)	gli uomini (the men)
lo zio (the uncle)	gli zii (the uncles)
lo spillo (the pin)	gli spilli (the pins)
la donna (the woman)	le donne (the women)
l'acqua (the water)	le acque (the waters)

The indefinite articles (*a, an*) are *un* or *uno* for masculine singular nouns and *una* for feminine singular nouns.

un fiume (a river)
una donna (a woman)

Adjectives vary in gender according to the nouns they modify. Notice the following:

un fiume lung*o* (a long river)
fiumi lungh*i* (long rivers)
una spiaggia lung*a* (a long beach)
spiagge lungh*e* (long beaches)

When a woman or girl speaks of herself or refers to another female, the feminine form of the adjective must be used:

Sono ammalato.	**I am sick.** (a man speaking)
Sono ammalata.	**I am sick.** (a woman speaking)
È ammalato.	**He is sick.**
È ammalata.	**She is sick.**
Sono ammalati.	**They are sick.** (men or men and women)
Sono ammalate.	**They are sick.** (women only)

Plurals The plurals of nouns and adjectives are formed by substituting -*i* for masculine singular -*o* and masculine and feminine singular -*e*. Feminine plurals substitute -*e* for singular -*a*.

mela (apple)	mele (apples)
dente (tooth)	denti (teeth)
libro (book)	libri (books)
arancia (orange)	arance (oranges)
ponte (bridge)	ponti (bridges)
matita (pencil)	matite (pencils)

Word Order The order of words in Italian is much the same as in English, with two prime exceptions. In Italian the adjective usually follows the noun:

un fiume lungo	**a long river**
lo spillo piccolo	**the small pin**
il vestito nero	**the black dress**

And the indirect and direct object pronouns, in an affirmative statement, precede the verb:

| He gave me the money. | Mi ha dato il denaro. |
| He gave it to me. | Me l'ha dato. |

Verbs Person is indicated in Italian verbs by endings attached to the verb stem. In regular verbs, the verb stem is got by dropping the -*are*, -*ere*, and -*ire* from the infinite form. (Some verb stems are irregular.) Notice the following:

parlare, **to speak**
parl*o*, **I speak**
parl*a*, **he, she speaks; you** (polite) **speak**
parl*iamo*, **we speak**
parl*ate*, **you** (pl., polite) **speak**
parl*ano*, **they speak**

prendere, **to take**
prend*o*, **I take**
prend*e*, **he, she takes; you** (polite) **take**
prend*iamo*, **we take**
prend*ete*, **you** (pl., polite) **take**
prend*ono*, **they take**

partire, **to leave**
part*o*, **I leave**
part*e*, **he, she leaves; you** (polite) **leave**
part*iamo*, **we leave**
part*ite*, **you** (pl., polite) **leave**
part*ono*, **they leave**

finire, **to finish**
fin*isco*, **I finish**
fin*isce*, **he, she finishes; you** (polite) **finish**
fin*iamo*, **we finish**
fin*ite*, **you** (pl., polite) **finish**
fin*iscono*, **they finish**

There is a set of personal subject pronouns that indicate person with verbs, but they are used largely for emphasis:

parlo, I speak   io parlo, *I* speak
ho parlato, I spoke   io ho parlato, *I* spoke
parlano, they speak   essi parlano, *they* speak

The reflexive pronouns used with reflexive verbs (those ending in *-si* in the Dictionary) follow the same rule for word order given above.

a, uno, una, un, un' *oo'-noh, oo'nah, oon, oon*
able: to be able, potere *poh-teh'-reh*
aboard, a bordo *ah bor'-doh*
about *adv.,* quasi *kwah'-zee*
about *prep.,* circa *cheer'-kah*
above, sopra *soh'-prah*
abroad, all'estero *ahl-les'-te-roh*
absolutely, assolutamente *ahs-soh-loo-tah-men'-teh*
accelerate, accelerare *ahch-cheh-leh-rah'-reh*
accelerator, acceleratore *ahch-cheh-leh-rah-toh'-reh*
accent *n.,* accento *ahch-chen'-toh*
accept *v.,* accettare *ahch-chet-tah'-reh* [31]
accident, incidente *een-chee-den'-teh* [14]
according to, secondo *seh-kon'-doh*
account *n.,* conto *kon'-toh*
ache *n.,* dolore *doh-loh'-reh*
ache *v.,* far male, dolere *fahr mah'-leh, doh-leh'-reh*
acquaintance, conoscenza *koh-noh-shehn'-tsah*
across, attraverso *aht-trah-ver'-soh*
act *n.,* atto *aht'-toh*
act [do] *v.,* agire, fare *ah-jee'-reh, fah'-reh*; [drama],
    recitare *reh-chee-tah'-reh*
active, attivo *aht-tee'-voh*
actor, attore *aht-toh'-reh*
actress, attrice *aht-tree'-cheh*
actual, attuale *aht-too-ah'-leh*
add, sommare, aggiungere *som-mah'-reh, ahj-joon'-geh-
    reh*
address *n.,* indirizzo *een-dee-reet'-tsoh* [30]
admiration, ammirazione (f) *ahm-mee-rah-tsyoh'-neh*
admire, ammirare *ahm-mee-rah'-reh*
admission, ammissione (f) *ahm-mees-syoh'-neh*
admit, ammettere *ahm-met'-teh-reh*
adorable, adorabile *ah-doh-rah'-bee-leh*
advance *v.,* avanzare *ah-vahn-tsah'-reh*
advantage, vantaggio *vahn-tahj'-joh*

adventure, avventura *ahv-ven-too'-rah*

advertisement, pubblicità *poob-blee-chee-tah'*

advice, consiglio *kon-seel'-yoh*

advise, consigliare *kon-seel-yah'-reh*

affectionate, affettuoso *ahf-fet-too-oh'-zoh*

afraid: to be afraid, aver paura *ah-vehr' pah-oo'-rah*

after, dopo *doh'-poh*

afternoon, pomeriggio *poh-meh-reej'-joh*

afterwards, dopo *doh'-poh*

again, di nuovo *dee nwoh'-voh*

against, contro *kon'-troh*

age, età *eh-tah'*

agent, agente *ah-jen'-teh*

ago, fa *fah*

agree: to be in accord, essere d'accordo *es'-seh-reh dahk-kor'-doh*

agreeable [pleasing], gradevole *grah-deh'-voh-leh*

agreement, accordo *ahk-kohr'-doh*

ahead: straight ahead, sempre diritto *sem'-preh dee-reet'-toh*

air, aria *ah'-ree-yah* [74]

air filter, filtro d'aria *feel'-troh dah'-ree-yah*

air line, linea aerea *lee'-neh-yah ah-eh'-reh-yah*

airmail, posta aerea *pos'-tah ah-eh'-reh-yah*

airplane, aereo, aeroplano *ah-eh'-reh-oh, ah-eh-roh-plah'-noh* [89, 90]

airport, aeroporto *ah-eh-roh-por'-toh* [45, 88]

alarm, allarme (m) *ahl-lahr'-meh*

alarm clock, sveglia *zvehl'-yah*

alcohol, alcool *ahl-koh-ohl'*

alike, simile, somigliante *see'-mee-leh, soh-meel-yahn'-teh*

alive, vivo *vee'-voh*

all, tutto *toot'-toh* **not at all** [none], niente affatto *nyen'-teh ahf-faht'-toh*; [it's nothing], non c'è di che *non che dee keh* **after all,** dopo tutto *doh'-poh toot'-toh*

allergy, allergia *ahl-ler-jee'-yah*

allow, permettere *per-met'-teh-reh*

almond, mandorla *mahn'-dor-lah*

almost, quasi *kwah'-zee*

alone, solo *soh'-loh*

along, lungo *loon'-goh*

already, già *jah* [57]

also, anche *ahn'-keh*

altar, altare (m) *ahl-tah'-reh*

alter, modificarsi *moh-dee-fee-kahr'-see*

alteration [of clothing], alterazione *ahl-teh-rah-tsyoh'-neh*

although, sebbene, benchè *seb-beh'-neh, ben-keh'*

altogether, interamente *een-teh-rah-men'-teh*

always, sempre *sem'-preh*

am: I am, sono, sto, io sono *soh'-noh, stoh, ee'-yoh soh'-noh*

ambassador, ambasciatore (m) *ahm-bah-shah-toh'-reh*

American, americano *ah-meh-ree-kah'-noh*

amount, somma *som'-mah*

amusement, divertimento *dee-ver-tee-men'-toh*

amusing, divertente *dee-ver-ten'-teh*

an, uno, una, un, un' *oo'-noh, oo'-nah, oon, oon*

and, e, ed *eh, ehd*

anger n., rabbia, collera *rahb'-byah, kol'-leh-rah*

angry, arrabbiato, adirato *ahr-rahb-byah'-toh, ah-dee-rah'-toh*

animal, animale (m) *ah-nee-mah'-leh*

ankle, caviglia *kah-veel'-yah*

announce, anunziare *ah-noon-tsyah'-reh*

annoy, annoiare *ahn-noh-yah'-reh*

another, un altro, un'altra *oon ahl'-troh, oon ahl'-trah*

answer n., risposta *rees-pos'-tah*

answer v., rispondere *rees-pon'-deh-reh* [42]

antique shop, negozio di antichità *neh-goh'-tsyoh dee ahn-tee-kee-tah'*

anxious, ansioso *ahn-syoh'-zoh*

any, alcuno *ahl-koo'-noh*
anyone, chiunque *kee-yoon'-kweh*
anyhow, comunque, in ogni modo *koh-moon'-kweh, een on'-yee moh'-doh*
anything, qualunque cosa, qualsiasi cosa *kwah-loon'-kweh ko'-zah, kwahl-see'-yah-zee ko'-zah*
anywhere, dovunque, ovunque *doh-voon'-kweh, oh-voon'-kweh*
apartment, appartamento *ahp-pahr-tah-men'-toh*
apologize, scusarsi *skoo-zahr'-see*
apology, apologia *ah-poh-loh-jee'-yah*
appear apparire *ahp-pah-ree'-reh*
appendicitis, appendicite *ahp-pen-dee-chee'-teh*
appendix, appendice *ahp-pen'-dee-cheh*
appetite, appetito *ahp-peh-tee'-toh*
appetizer, antipasto *ahn-tee-pahs'-toh*
apple, mela *meh'-lah*
appointment, appuntamento *ahp-poon-tah-men'-toh*
appreciate, apprezzare *ahp-pret-tsah'-reh*
approve, approvare *ahp-proh-vah'-reh*
approximately, approssimativamente *ahp-pros-see-mah-tee-vah-men'-teh*
April, aprile *ah-pree'-leh*
arch, arco *ahr'-koh*
architect, architetto *ahr-kee-tet'-toh*
architecture, architettura *ahr-kee-tet-too'-rah*
are: you are, tu sei, Lei è *too say, leh'-ee e* **you** (pl), **they are,** voi siete, essi sono *voy syeh'-teh, es'-see soh'-noh* **we are,** noi siamo *noy syah'-moh*
area, area *ah'-reh-yah*
argue, disputare *dees-poo-tah'-reh*
arm, braccio *brahch'-choh*
around, intorno *een-tor'-noh*
arrange, regolare *reh-goh-lah'-reh*
arrest *v.,* arrestare *ahr-res-tah'-reh*
arrival, arrivo *ahr-ree'-voh* [85]

arrive, arrivare *ahr-ree-vah'-reh* [25, 46, 85, 87, 88, 90]
art, arte (f) *ahr'-teh* [99]
artichoke, carciofo *kahr-choh'-foh*
article, articolo *ahr-tee'-koh-loh*
artificial, artificiale *ahr-tee-fee-chah'-leh*
artist, artista *ahr-tees'-tah*
as, come *ko'-meh*
ashamed, vergognoso *ver-gon-yoh'-zoh*
ashore, a terra *ah ter'-rah* [88]
ashtray, portacenere (m) *por-tah-cheh'-neh-reh* [50]
ask, domandare *doh-mahn-dah'-reh*
asleep, addormentato *ahd-dor-men-tah'-toh*
asparagus, asparagi (m, pl) *ahs-pah'-rah-jee*
aspirin, aspirina *ahs-pee-ree'-nah*
assist, assistere *ahs-sees'-teh-reh*
assistant, assistente *ahs-sees-ten'-teh*
associate *n.,* socio *soh'-choh*
association, associazione (f) *ahs-soh-chah-tsyoh'-neh*
assure, assicurare *ahs-see-koo-rah'-reh*
at *prep.,* a, ad *ah, ahd*
Atlantic, Atlantico *aht-lahn'-tee-koh*
attach, accludere *ahk-kloo'-deh-reh*
attain [reach], ottenere *ot-teh-neh'-reh*
attempt *v.,* provare, tentare *proh-vah'-reh, ten-tah'-reh*
attend, attendere, assistere *aht-ten'-deh-reh, ahs-sees'-teh-reh*
attention, attenzione (f) *aht-ten-tsyoh'-neh*
attract, attirare *aht-tee-rah'-reh*
audience, udienza *oo-dyen'-tsah*
August, agosto *ah-gos'-toh*
aunt, zia *dzee'-yah*
author, autore (m) *ow-toh'-reh*
authority, autorità *ow-toh-ree-tah'*
automobile, automobile (f), macchina *ow-toh-moh'-bee-leh, mahk'-kee-nah*
autumn, autunno *ow-toon'-noh*

available, disponibile *dees-poh-nee'-bee-leh*
avenue, via, viale (m) *vee'-yah, vee-yah'-leh*
avoid, evitare *eh-vee-tah'-reh*
await, aspettare *ah-spet-tah'-reh*
awake *adj.*, sveglio *zvehl'-yoh*
awake *v.*, svegliarsi *zvehl-yahr'-see*
away, via, lontano *vee'-yah, lon-tah'-noh*
axle, asse (f) *ahs'-seh*

baby, bambino, bimbo *bahm-bee'-noh, beem'-boh*
bachelor, celibe (m) *cheh'-lee-beh*
back *adv.*, dietro *dyeh'-troh* **to go back,** tornare *tohr-
    nah'-reh*
back *n.*, schiena *skyeh'-nah*
bacon, pancetta, lardo *pahn-chet'-tah, lahr'-doh*
bad, cattivo *kaht-tee'-voh*
badly, male *mah'-leh*
bag, sacco, borsa *sahk'-koh, bor'-sah*; [suitcase], valigia
    vah-lee'-jah [34, 83]
baggage, bagaglio *bah-gahl'-yoh* [83]
baggage check, scontrino *skon-tree'-noh* [83]
bakery, panetteria *pah-net-teh-ree'-yah*
balcony, galleria, balcone (m) *gahl-leh-ree'-yah, bahl-koh'-
    neh*
ball, palla *pahl'-lah*
banana, banana *bah-nah'-nah*
band [music], banda *bahn'-dah*
bandage, benda *ben'-dah*
bank, banca *bahn'-kah* [30]
bar, bar (m) *bahr*
barber, barbiere (m) *bahr-byeh'-reh*
bargain *n.*, occasione (f) *ok-kah-zyoh'-neh*
basket, cestino *ches-tee'-noh*
bath, bagno *bahn'-yoh* [37]
bathe, bagnarsi, fare il bagno *bahn-yahr'-see, fah'-reh eel
    bahn'-yoh*

bathing suit, costume da bagno (m) *kos-too'-meh dah bahn'-yoh*

bathroom, stanza da bagno *stahn'-tsah dah bahn'-yoh* [39]

battery, batteria *baht-teh-ree'-yah*

bay, baia *bah'-yah*

be, essere, stare *es'-seh-reh, stah'-reh*

beach, spiaggia *spyahj'-jah* [102]

beans, fagioli *fah-joh'-lee*

beard, barba *bahr'-bah*

beautiful, bello *behl'-loh* [10]

beauty parlor, salone di bellezza *sah-loh'-neh dee bel-leht'-tsah*

because, perchè *per-keh'*

become, diventare *dee-ven-tah'-reh*

bed, letto *let'-toh* [94]   **to go to bed**, andare al letto *ahn-dah'-reh ahl let'-toh*

bedroom, camera da letto *kah'-meh-rah dah let'-toh*

bee, ape (f) *ah'-peh*

beef, manzo *mahn'-dzoh*

beefsteak, bistecca *bee-stek'-kah*

beer, birra *beer'-rah* [56]

beet, barbabietola *bahr-bah-byeh'-toh-lah*

before [time], prima (di) *pree'-mah (dee)*; [place], davanti a *dah-vahn'-tee ah*

begin, cominciare *ko-meen-chah'-reh*

beginning, principio *preen-chee'-pyoh*

behind, dietro a *dyeh'-troh ah*

believe, credere *kreh'-deh-reh*

bell, campana *kahm-pah'-nah*

belong, appartenere *ahp-pahr-teh-neh'-reh*

belt, cintura *cheen-too'-rah* [73, 89]

beside, accanto a, al lato di *ahk-kahn'-toh ah, ahl lah'-toh dee*

besides, inoltre, di più *een-ohl'-treh, dee pyoo*

best, ottimo *ot'-tee-moh*

better *adj.*, migliore *meel-yoh'-reh*
better *adv.*, meglio *mehl'-yoh*
between, tra, fra *trah, frah*
big, grande, grosso *grahn'-deh, gros'-soh* [69]
bill, conto *kon'-toh* [57]
bird, uccello *ooch-chel'-loh*
birth, nascita *nah'-shee-tah*
birthday, compleanno *kom-pleh-ahn'-noh*
bit: a bit, un poco *oon poh'-koh*
bite *v.*, mordere *mor'-deh-reh*
black, nero *neh'-roh*
blanket, coperta *koh-per'-tah*
bleed, sanguinare *sahn-gwee-nah'-reh* [93]
blind, cieco *chyeh'-koh*
blister, bolla *bol'-lah*
block *n.*, masso *mahs'-soh*
blonde, biondo *byon'-doh*
blood, sangue (m) *sahn'-gweh*
blouse, blusa, camicetta *bloo'-zah, kah-mee-chet'-tah*
blue, azzurro *ahd-dzoor'-roh*
board; room and board, camera con vitto *kah'-meh-rah kon veet'-toh*
boarding house, pensione (f) *pen-syoh'-neh*
boarding pass, permesso d'imbarco *per-mes'-soh deem-bahr'-koh* [89]
boat, barca *bahr'-kah* [101]
body, corpo *kor'-poh*
boil *v.*, bollire *bol-lee'-reh*
bone, osso *os'-soh*
book, libro *leeb'-roh*
bookstore, libreria *leeb-reh-ree'-yah*
booth, cabina *kah-bee'-nah*
boot, stivale (m) *stee-vah'-leh*
border *n.*, frontiera, confine (m) *fron-tyeh'-rah, kon-fee'-neh*

born, nato *nah'-toh*

borrow, prendere a prestito *pren'-deh-reh ah pres'-tee-toh*

both, tutti e due (m), tutte e due (f) *toot'-tee eh doo'-eh, toot'-teh eh doo'-eh*

bottle, bottiglia *bot-teel'-yah* [55, 56]

bottle opener, cavatappi (m) *kah-vah-tahp'-pee*

bottom, fondo *fon'-doh*

box, scatola *skah'-toh-lah* [34]

boy, ragazzo *rah-gaht'-tsoh*

bracelet, braccialetto *brahch-chah-let'-toh*

brake *n.*, freno *freh'-noh*

brandy, acquavite (m), cognac *ahk-kwah-vee'-teh, kon-yahk'*

brassiere, reggipetto *rej-jee-pet'-toh*

brave, coraggioso *koh-rahj-joh'-zoh*

bread, pane (m) *pah'-neh*

break *v.*, rompere *rom'-peh-reh*

breakfast, prima colazione (f) *pree'-mah koh-lah-tsyoh'-neh* [38, 48, 50, 52]

breast, seno *seh'-noh*

breath, respiro *res-pee'-roh*

breathe, respirare *res-pee-rah'-reh*

bridge, ponte (m) *pon'-teh* [101]

bright, chiaro *kyah'-roh*

bring, portare *por-tah'-reh* [13, 50, 51, 55]

broken, rotto *rot'-toh*

brother, fratello *frah-tel'-loh* [3]

brown, marrone, bruno *mahr-roh'-neh, broo'-noh*

bruise *n.*, bernoccolo *ber-nok'-koh-loh*

brush *n.*, spazzola *spaht'-tsoh-lah*

brunette, bruno *broo'-noh*

build *v.*, costruire *kos-troo-ee'-reh*

building, edifizio *eh-dee-fee'-tsyoh*

burn *n.*, bruciatura *broo-chah-too'-rah*

burn *v.*, bruciare *broo-chah'-reh* [94]

burst, scoppiare *skop-pyah'-reh*
bus, autobus, pullman *ow'-toh-boos, pool'-mahn* [15, 46]
business, affari (m, pl) *ahf-fah'-ree*
busy, occupato *ok-koo-pah'-toh* [43]
but, ma *mah*
butter, būrro *boor'-roh* [49, 50, 51]
button, bottone (m) *bot-toh'-neh*
buy, comprare *kom-prah'-reh* [66, 70]
by, da *dah*

cabbage, cavolo *kah'-voh-loh*
cabin, cabina *kah-bee'-nah* [86, 87]
café, caffè (m) *kahf-feh'*
cake, torta *tor'-tah*
call *n.*, chiamata *kyah-mah'-tah* [41, 42]
call *v.*, chiamare *kyah-mah'-reh* [15, 40, 44]
camera, macchina fotografica *mahk'-kee-nah foh-toh-grah'-fee-kah*
can *n.*, latta *laht'-tah*
can: to be able, potere *poh-teh'-reh* **I can**, posso *pos'-soh*
canal, canale (m) *kah-nah'-leh*
cancel *v.*, annullare *ahn-nool-lah'-reh*
candy, caramella, dolci *kah-rah-mel'-lah, dol'-chee*
candy store, confetteria *kon-fet-teh-ree'-yah*
capital, capitale (f) *kah-pee-tah'-leh*
car, automobile (f), macchina *ow-toh-moh'-bee-leh, mahk'-kee-nah* [72, 73, 74, 76]
carburetor, carburatore (m) *kahr-boo-rah-toh'-reh*
card, cartolina *kahr-toh-lee'-nah*
care, *n.*, cura *koo'-rah*
care *v.*, preoccuparsi (di) *preh-ok-koo-pahr'-see (dee)*
careful, cauto *kow'-toh*
carpet, tappeto *tahp-peh'-toh*
carrot, carota *kah-roh'-tah*
carry, portare *por-tah'-reh* [35]
cash *n.*, denaro contante *deh-nah'-roh kon-tahn'-teh* [70]

cashier, cassiere (m) *kahs-syeh'-reh* [57]

castle, castello *kahs-tehl'-loh* [101]

cat, gatto *gaht'-toh*

catch *v.,* prendere, acchiappare *pren'-deh-reh, ahk-kyahp-pah'-reh*

cathedral, cattedrale (f), duomo *kaht-teh-drah'-leh, dwoh'-moh* [100]

Catholic, cattolico *kaht-toh'-lee-koh*

catsup, salsa di pomodori *sahl'-sah dee poh-moh-doh'-ree*

cattle, bestiame (m) *bes-tee-yah'-meh*

cauliflower, cavolfiore (m) *kah-vol-fyoh'-reh*

caution, precauzione (f) *preh-kow-tsyoh'-neh*

cave, caverna, grotta *kah-ver'-nah, grot'-tah*

ceiling, soffitto *sof-feet'-toh*

celery, sedano *seh'-dah-noh*

cellar, cantina *kahn-tee'-nah*

cemetary, cimitero *chee-mee-teh'-roh*

center, centro *chen'-troh*

centimeter, centimetro *chen-tee'-meh-troh*

century, secolo *seh'-koh-loh*

ceremony, cerimonia *cheh-ree-moh-nee'-yah*

certain, certo *cher'-toh*

certainly, certo *cher'-toh*

chair, sedia *seh'-dyah* [87]

chambermaid, cameriera *kah-me-ree-yeh'-rah* [40]

champagne, sciampagna *shahm-pahn'-yah*

chance *n.,* caso, azzardo *kah'-zoh, ahd-dzahr'-doh*

change [coins], cambio *kahm'-byoh* [32]

change *v.,* cambiare *kahm-byah'-reh* [31, 32]

chapel, cappella *kahp-pehl'-lah*

charge *v.,* mettere sul conto *met'-teh-reh sool kon'-toh*

charming, grazioso, incantevole *grah-tsyoh'-zoh, een-kahn-teh'-voh-leh*

chauffeur, autista (m) *ow-tees'-tah*

cheap, a buon mercato *ah bwon mer-kah'-toh* [67]

check *n.*, assengo *ahs-sehn'-yoh* [31] **traveler's check**, assegno di viaggio *ahs-sehn'-yoh dee vyahj'-joh* [31]

check [one's luggage], spedire una valigia *speh-dee'-reh oo'-nah vah-lee'-jah* [83]

check [inspect], esaminare, verificare *eh-zah-mee-nah'-reh, veh-ree-fee-kah'-reh* [76]

cheek, guancia *gwahn'-chah·*

cheese, formaggio *fohr-mahj'-joh*

cherry, ciliegia *chee-lee-yeh'-jah*

chest, petto *pet'-toh*

chicken, pollo *pol'-loh*

child, bambino, fanciullo *bahm-bee'-noh, fahn-chool'-loh*

chin, mento *men'-toh*

chocolate, cioccolata *chok-koh-lah'-tah*

choose, scegliere *shehl'-yeh-reh*

chop, costoletta *kos-toh-let'-tah*

Christmas, Natale (m) *nah-tah'-leh*

church, chiesa *kyeh'-zah* [99, 100]

cigar, sigaro *see'-gah-roh*

cigarette, sigaretta *see-gah-ret'-tah* [34, 70]

cinema, cinema *chee'-neh-mah*

circle, circolo *cheer'-koh-loh*

citizen, cittadino *cheet-tah-dee'-noh*

city, città *cheet-tah'* [99, 100, 101]

class, classe (f) *klahs'-seh* **first class**, prima classe *pree'-mah klahs'-seh* **second class**, seconda classe *seh-kon'-dah klahs'-seh*

classify, classificare *klahs-see-fee-kah'-reh*

clean *adj.*, pulito *poo-lee'-toh* [40, 55, 56]

clean *v.*, pulire *poo-lee'-reh*

cleaners, lavanderia a secco *lah-vahn-deh-ree'-yah ah sek'-koh*

clear, chiaro *kyah'-roh*

climb, salire, arrampicarsi *sah-lee'-reh, ahr-rahm-pee-kahr'-see*

clock, orologio *oh-roh-lohj'-joh*
close [near], vicino *vee-chee'-noh*
close *v.*, chiudere *kyoo'-deh-reh* [34, 39, 62, 84, 99, 100]
closed, chiuso *kyoo'-zoh* [99, 100]
closet, armadio *ahr-mah'-dyoh*
cloth, tela *teh'-lah*
clothes, vestiti *ves-tee'-tee*
cloud, nuvola *noo'-voh-lah* [7]
clutch [of a car], frizione (f) *free-tsyoh'-neh*
coast, costa *kos'-tah*
coat, cappotto, soprabito *kahp-pot'-toh, soh-prah'-bee-toh*
cocktail, cocktail *kok'-tehl*
coffee, caffè (m) *kahf-feh'* [49, 50, 51, 53]
cognac, cognac (m) *kon-yahk'*
coin, moneta *moh-neh'-tah* [42]
cold *adj.*, freddo *frehd'-doh* [51, 52]   **I am cold,** ho freddo *oh frehd'-doh*   **it is cold,** fa freddo *fah frehd'-doh*
cold *n.*, raffreddore (m) *rahf-frehd-doh'-reh* [96]
collar, colletto *kol-let'-toh*
collect, raccogliere *rahk-kohl'-yeh-reh*
collection, collezione (f) *kol-leh-tsyoh'-neh*
college, università, collegio *oo-nee-ver-see-tah', kol-lehj'-joh*
collide, scontrarsi *skon-trahr'-see*
color, colore (m) *koh-loh'-reh* [68]
comb, pettine (m) *pet'-tee-neh*
come, venire *veh-nee'-reh* [12, 96, 97]
comfortable, comodo *koh'-moh-doh*
company, compagnia, ditta *kom-pahn-yee'-yah, deet'-tah*
comparison, paragone (m), confronto *pah-rah'-goh-neh, kon-fron'-toh*
compartment, compartimento *kom-pahr-tee-men'-toh*
complain, lamentarsi, lagnarsi *lah-men-tahr'-see, lahn-yahr'-see*
complete *adj.*, completo *kom-pleh'-toh*

compliment *n*., complimento *kom-plee-men'-toh*
concert, concerto *kon-cher'-toh*
condition, condizione (f) *kon-dee-tsyoh'-neh*
confuse, confondere *kon-fon'-deh-reh*
congratulations, congratulazioni (f, pl) *kon-grah-too-lah-tsyoh'-nee*
connect, connettere *kon-net'-teh-reh*
consent *v*., consentire *kon-sen-tee'-reh*
consider, considerare *kon-see-deh-rah'-reh*
constipated, costipato *kos-tee-pah'-toh*
consul, console (m) *kon'-soh-leh*
consulate, consolato *kon-soh-lah'-toh*
contagious, contagioso *kon-tah-joh'-zoh*
contain, contenere *kon-teh-neh'-reh*
contented, contento *kon-ten'-toh*
continue, continuare *kon-tee-noo-ah'-reh*
contrary, contrario *kon-trah'-ree-yoh* **on the contrary,** al contrario *ahl kon-trah'-ree-yoh*
convenient, conveniente *kon-veh-nyen'-teh*
conversation, conversazione (f) *kon-ver-sah-tsyoh'-neh*
cook *n*., cuoco *kwoh'-koh*
cook *v*., cuocere *kwoh'-cheh-reh*
cool, fresco *fres'-koh* [8]
copy, copia *koh'-pyah*
corkscrew, cavatappi (m) *kah-vah-tahp'-pee*
corn, frumento *froo-men'-toh*
corner, angolo *ahn'-goh-loh*
correct *adj*., corretto *kor-ret'-toh*
cost *n*., costo *kos'-toh*
cost *v*., costare *kos-tah'-reh* [67, 72]
cotton, cotone (m) *koh-toh'-neh*
cough *n*., tosse (f) *tos'-seh*
cough *v*., tossire *tos-see'-reh* [96]
count *v*., contare *kon-tah'-reh* [32]
country [nation], paese (m) *pah-eh'-zeh* [73]; [not city], campagna *kahm-pahn'-yah*

courage, coraggio *koh-rahj-joh*
course, corso *kor'-soh* **of course,** certo *cher'-toh* **main course,** piatto principale *pyaht'-toh preen-chee-pah'-leh*
court, tribunale (m) *tree-boo-nah'-leh*
courtyard, cortile (m) *kor-tee'-leh* [37]
cover *v.,* coprire *koh-pree'-reh*
cow, vacca, mucca *vahk'-kah, mook'-kah*
crab, granchio *grahn'-kyoh*
cramp, crampo *krahm'-poh*
crazy, pazzo, matto *paht'-tsoh, maht'-toh*
cream, crema, panna *kreh'-mah, pahn'-nah*
cross *n.,* croce (f) *kroh'-cheh*
cross *v.,* attraversare *aht-trah-ver-sah'-reh* [101]
crossing, incrocio *een-kroh'-choh;* [by ship], traversata *trah-ver-sah'-tah*
crossroads, incrocio, bivio *een-kroh'-choh, bee'-vee-yoh*
crowd, folla *fol'-lah*
cry *v.,* piangere *pyahn-jeh'-reh*
cucumber, cetriolo *cheh-tree-yoh'-loh*
cup, tazza *taht'-tsah* [53]
curve, curva *koor'-vah*
custard, crema *kreh'-mah*
customer, cliente (m) *klee-yen'-teh*
customs, dogana *doh-gah'-nah*
cut [injury], piaga *pyah'-gah*
cut *v.,* tagliare *tahl-yah'-reh*
cutlet, costoletta *kos-toh-let'-tah*

daily *adj.,* quotidiano *kwoh-tee-dyah'-noh*
daily *adv.,* ogni giorno *oh'-nyee johr'-noh*
damage *v.,* danneggiare *dahn-nehj-jah'-reh*
damaged, danneggiato *dahn-nehj-jah'-toh*
damp, umido *oo'-mee-doh* [8]
dance *n.,* ballo *bahl'-loh*
dance *v.,* ballare *bahl-lah'-reh*
danger, pericolo *peh-ree'-koh-loh*

dangerous, pericoloso *peh-ree-koh-loh'-zoh*

dare *v.,* osare *oh-zah'-reh*

dark, scuro, buio *skoo'-roh, boo'-ee-yoh*

darkness, oscurità *oh-skoo-ree-tah'*

date [time], data *dah'-tah;* [appointment], appuntamento *ahp-poon-tah-men'-toh*

daughter, figlia *feel'-yah* [3]

day, giorno *johr'-noh* **per day, a day,** al giorno *ahl johr'-noh*

dead, morto *mor'-toh*

dear [endearment], caro *kah'-roh*

December, dicembre *dee-chem'-breh*

decide, decidere *deh-chee'-deh-reh*

deck, ponte *pon'-teh* [87]

declare, dichiarare *dee-kyah-rah'-reh* [33]

deep, profondo *proh-fon'-doh*

deer, cervo *cher'-voh*

delay *n.,* ritardo *ree-tahr'-doh* [90]

delicious, delizioso *deh-lee-tsyoh'-zoh*

delighted, felicissimo *feh-lee-chees'-see-moh*

deliver, consegnare *kon-sehn-yah'-reh*

dentist, dentista (m) *den-tees'-tah*

deodorant, deodorante (m) *deh-oh-doh-rahn'-teh*

department store, grande magazzino *grahn'-deh mah-gahd-dzee'-noh*

departure, partenza *pahr-tehn'-tsah* [85]

deposit *v.,* depositare *deh-poh-zee-tah'-reh* [42]

descend, scendere *shen'-deh-reh*

describe, descrivere *deh-skree'-veh-reh*

desert *n.,* deserto *deh-zer'-toh*

desert *v.,* disertare, abbandonare *dee-zer-tah'-reh, ahb-bahn-doh-nah'-reh*

desire *v.,* desiderare *deh-zee-deh-rah'-reh*

desk, scrivania *skree-vah-nee'-yah*

dessert, dessert, dolci *dehs-ser', dohl'-chee* [56]

destroy, distruggere *dee-strooj'-jeh-reh*

detour, deviazione (f) *deh-vee-yah-tsyoh'-neh*

develop, sviluppare *zvee-loop-pah'-reh*

dial *v*., fare il numero *fah'-reh eel noo'-meh-roh* [42, 43]

diamond, diamante (m) *dee-yah-mahn'-teh*

diaper, pannilino *pahn-nee-lee'-noh*

diarrhea, diarrea *dee-yahr-reh'-yah*

dictionary, dizionario *dee-tsee-yoh-nah'-ree-yoh*

die, morire *moh-ree'-reh*

difference, differenza *deef-feh-rehn'-tsah*

different, differente *deef-feh-rehn'-teh*

difficult, difficile *deef-fee'-chee-leh*

dine, pranzare *prahn-dzah'-reh* [53]

dining car, carrozza ristorante *kahr-rot'-tsah rees-toh-rahn'-teh* [84]

dining room, sala da pranzo *sah'-lah dah prahn'-dzoh* [38, 87]

dinner, pranzo *prahn'-dzoh* [48, 50]

direct, diretto *dee-ret'-toh*

direction, direzione (f) *dee-reh-tsyoh'-neh*

director, direttore (m) *dee-reht-toh'-reh*

dirty, sporco *spor'-koh* [55]

disappear, sparire *spah-ree'-reh*

discount *n*., sconto *skon'-toh* [70]

discuss, discutere *dee-skoo'-teh-reh*

disease, malattia *mah-laht-tee'-yah*

dish, piatto *pyaht'-toh*

disinfect, disinfettare *dee-seen-fet'-tah'-reh*

distance, distanza *dee-stahn'-tsah*

district, distretto *dee-stret'-toh*

disturb, disturbare *dee-stoor-bah'-reh*

divorced, divorziato *dee-vohr-tsyah'-toh*

do, fare *fah'-reh*   **how do you do?** come sta? *ko'-meh stah*

dock, molo *moh'-loh*

doctor, medico, dottore *meh'-dee-koh, dot-toh'-reh* [51, 91]

dog, cane (m) *kah'-neh*

doll, bambola *bahm'-boh-lah*

dollar, dollaro *dol'-lah-roh* [31]
done, fatto *faht'-toh*
donkey, asino *ah'-zee-noh*
door, porta *por'-tah*
dose, dose (f) *doh'-zeh*
double, doppio *dop'-pyoh*
doubt, dubbio *doob'-byoh* **without doubt,** senza dubbio *sehn'-tsah doob'-byoh* **no doubt,** nessun dubbio *nes-soon' doob'-byoh*
down, giù *joo* **to go down,** scendere *shen'-deh-reh*
downtown, centro città *chen'-troh chee-tah'* [46]
dozen, dozzina *dod-dzee'-nah*
drawer, cassetto *kahs-set'-toh*
dress *n.,* vestito *ves-tee'-toh* [68]
dress [oneself], vestirsi *ves-teer'-see*
dressmaker, sarta *sahr'-tah*
drink *n.,* bibita, bevanda *bee'-bee-tah, beh-vahn'-dah*
drink *v.,* bere *beh'-reh*
drive *v.,* condurre *kon-door'-reh* [45, 75, 76]
driver, autista *ow-tees'-tah* [44]
drop *v.,* lasciar cadere *lah-shar' kah-deh'-reh*
druggist, farmacista (m) *fahr-mah-chees'-tah*
drugstore, farmacia *fahr-mah-chee'-yah* [92]
drunk, ubriaco *oo-bree-yah'-koh*
dry, secco *sek'-koh*
duck, anitra *ah'-nee-trah*
during, durante *doo-rahn'-teh*
dust, polvere (f) *pol'-veh-reh*
duty, dovere (m) *doh-veh'-reh* [34]
dysentery, dissenteria *dees-sen-teh-ree'-yah*

each ciascuno, ciascun *chahs-koo'-noh, chahs-koon'*
each one, ciascuno *chahs-koo'-noh*
eager, avido *ah'-vee-doh*
ear, orecchio *oh-rek'-kyoh*
earache, mal d'orecchi *mahl doh-rek'-kee*

early, presto, di buon'ora *pres'-toh, dee bwon-oh'-rah* [24]
earn, guadagnare *gwah-dahn-yah'-reh*
earrings, orecchini *oh-rek-kee'-nee*
earth, terra *ter'-rah*
easily, facilmente *fah-cheel-men'-teh*
east, est (m) *est*
Easter, Pasqua *pahs'-kwah*
easy, facile *fah'-chee-leh*
eat, mangiare *mahn-jah'-reh* [38, 48, 52, 56, 87]
edge, orlo *ohr'-loh*
egg, uovo *woh'-voh*
eight, otto *ot'-toh*
eighteen, diciotto *dee-chot'-toh*
eighth, ottavo *ot-tah'-voh*
eighty, ottanta *ot-tahn'-tah*
either, l'uno o l'altro *loo'-noh oh lahl'-troh*
either . . . or . . . , o . . . o . . . *oh . . . oh . . .*
elbow, gomito *goh'-mee-toh*
electric, elettrico *eh-let'-tree-koh*
elevator, ascensore (m) *ah-shen-soh'-reh* [39]
eleven, undici *oon'-dee-chee*
else: nobody else, nessun altro *nes-soon' ahl'-troh* **nothing else**, nient'altro *nyent-ahl'-troh* **something else**, qualcosa d'altro *kwahl-ko'-zah dahl'-troh*
elsewhere, altrove *ahl-troh'-veh*
embark, imbarcarsi *eem-bahr-kahr'-see*
embarrassed, imbarazzato *eem-bah-rahd-dzah'-toh*
embassy, ambasciata *ahm-bah-shah'-tah*
embrace *v.*, abbracciare *ahb-brach-chah'-reh*
emergency, emergenza *eh-mer-jehn'-tsah*
empty, vuoto *vwoh'-toh*
end *n.*, fine (f) *fee'-neh*
engaged [busy], occupato *ok-koo-pah'-toh*
engine, motore (m) *moh-toh'-reh*
English, inglese *een-gleh'-zeh* [11]
enjoy godere *goh-deh'-reh*

enormous, enorme *eh-nohr'-meh*

enough, abbastaza *ahb-bahs-tahn'-tsah* **that's enough,** basta *bahs-tah*

enter, entrare *en-trah-reh*

entertaining, divertente *dee-ver-ten'-teh*

entire, intero *een-teh'-roh*

entrance, entrata, ingresso *en-trah'-tah, een-gres'-soh*

envelope, busta *boos'-tah*

equal, uguale *oo-gwah'-leh*

equipment, equipaggiamento *eh-kwee-pahj-jah-men'-toh*

error, errore (m) *er-roh'-reh*

Europe, Europa *eh-oo-roh'-pah*

even *adv.*, anche, perfino *ahn'-keh, per-fee'-noh*

even [number], pari *pah'-ree*

evening, sera *seh'-rah* [100] **good evening,** buona sera *bwoh'-nah seh'-rah*

ever, sempre, mai *sem'-preh, mah'-ee*

every, ogni *ohn'-yee*

everyone, ognuno *ohn-yoo'-noh*

everything, ogni cosa, tutto *ohn'-yee ko'-zah, toot'-toh*

everywhere, dappertutto *dahp-per-toot'-toh*

evidently, evidentemente *eh-vee-den-teh-men'-teh*

exact, esatto *eh-zaht'-toh*

examination, esame (m) *eh-zah'-meh*

examine, esaminare *eh-zah-mee-nah'-reh*

example, esempio *eh-zem'-pyoh* **for example,** per esempio *per eh-zem'-pyoh*

excellent, eccellente *ech-chel-len'-teh*

except, eccetto *ech-chet'-toh*

exchange *v.*, cambiare, scambiare *kahm-byah'-reh, skahm-byah'-reh*

exchange rate, cambio *kahm'-byoh* [31]

excursion, escursione (f) *es-koor-zyoh'-neh*

excuse *v.*, scusare *skoo-záh'-reh* **excuse me,** (mi) scusi *(mee) skoo'-zee*

exercise, esercizio *eh-zer-chee'-tsyoh*

exhibition, esposizione (f) *es-poh-zee-tsyoh'-neh* [99]
exit, uscita *oo-shee'-tah*
expect, sperare *speh-rah'-reh* [32]
expensive, costoso, caro *kos-toh'-zoh, kah'-roh* [38, 67]
explain, spiegare *spyeh-gah'-reh*
explanation, spiegazione (f) *spyeh-gah-tsyoh'-neh*
export *v.*, esportare *es-por-tah'-reh*
express *adj.*, espresso *es-pres'-soh*
extra, extra, suppletivo *es'-trah, soop-pleh-tee'-voh*
extraordinary, straordinario *strah-ohr-dee-nah'-ree-yoh*
eye, occhio *ok'-kyoh*

face, faccia, viso *fahch-chah, vee'-zoh*
factory, fabbrica *fahb'-bree-kah*
faint *v.*, svenire *zveh-nee'-reh*
fair [market], fiera *fyeh'-rah*
fall [season], autunno *ow-toon'-noh*
fall *n.*, caduta *kah-doo'-tah*
fall *v.*, cadere *kah-deh'-reh*
false, falso *fahl'-soh*
family, famiglia *fah-meel'-yah*
famous, famoso *fah-moh'-zoh*
fan, ventilatore (m), ventaglio *ven-tee-lah-toh'-reh, ven-tahl'-yoh*
far, lontano *lon-tah'-noh* **so far,** cosi lontano *ko-see' lon-tah'-noh* **how far is it?** a quanta distanza è? *ah kwahn'-tah dees-tahn'-tsah eh*?
fare [cost], tariffa *tah-reef'-fah* [45]
farewell, addio *ahd-dee'-yoh*
farm, podere (m), fattoria *poh-deh'-reh, faht-toh-ree'-yah*
farmer, agricoltore (m) *ah-gree-kol-toh'-reh*
farther, più lontano *pyoo lon-tah'-noh*
fashion, moda *moh'-dah*
fast [quick], veloce *veh-loh'-cheh*
fasten, attaccare *aht-tahk-kah'-reh* [89]

fat, grasso *grahs'-soh*
father, padre *pah'-dreh* [3]
father-in-law, suocero *swoh'-cheh-roh*
fault, colpa *kol'-pah*
favor, favore (m) *fah-voh'-reh*
favorite *adj. & n.*, favorito *fah-voh-ree'-toh*
fear: to be afraid, temere, aver paura *teh-meh'-reh, ah-vehr' pah-oo'-rah*
feather, piuma, penna *pyoo'-mah, pen'-nah*
February, febbraio *feb-brah'-yoh*
fee, onorario *oh-noh-rah'-ree-yoh*
feel, sentire *sen-tee'-reh* [92]
feeling, sentimento *sen-tee-men'-toh*
female, femmina *fem'-mee-nah*
fence, steccato *stek-kah'-toh*
fender, parafango *pah-rah-fahn'-goh*
ferry [boat], nave-traghetto *nah'-veh trah-get'-toh*
fever, febbre (f) *feb'-breh* [93]
few, pochi, poche *poh'-kee, poh'-keh*
field, campo *kahm'-poh*
fifteen, quindici *kween'-dee-chee*
fifth, quinto *kween'-toh*
fifty, cinquanta *cheen-kwahn'-tah*
fight *n.*, lotta *lot'-tah*
fight *v.*, combattere *kom-baht'-teh-reh*
fill *v.*, riempire *ree-em-pee'-reh* [39, 74]
filling [for a tooth], piombatura *pyom-bah-too'-rah*
film, pellicola, film *pel-lee'-koh-lah, feelm*
final, finale *fee-nah'-leh*
finally, finalmente *fee-nah'-men'-teh*
find, trovare *troh-vah'-reh*
fine *adj.*, bene *beh'-neh*
fine *n.*, multa *mool'-tah* [75]
finger, dito *dee'-toh* [93]
finish *v.*, finire *fee-nee'-reh*
fire, fuoco *fwoh'-koh* [15]

first, primo *pree'-moh*   **first class,** prima classe *pree'-mah klahs'-seh* [83, 87]

fish, pesce (m) *peh'-sheh* [56]

fish v., pescare *pes-kah'-reh*

fish-bone, lisca *lees'-kah*

fit [seizure], convulsione (f) *kon-vool-syoh'-neh*

fit v., andar bene *ahn-dahr' beh'-neh*

fitting [of a garment], prova *proh'-vah*

five, cinque *cheen'-kweh*

fix v., reparare, aggiustare *reh-pah-rah-reh, ahj-joos-tah'-reh* [74, 76]

flag, bandiera *bahn-dyeh'-rah*

flashbulb, lampadina fotografica *lahm-pah-dee'-nah fot-toh-grah'-fee-kah*

flat, piano *pyah'-noh*

flat tire, gomma forata *gom'-mah foh-rah'-tah* [74]

flavor, sapore (m) *sah-poh'-reh*

flight, volo *voh'-loh* [88, 89, 90]

flint, pietra focaia *pyeh'-trah foh-kah'-yah*

flirt v., civettare *chee-vet-tah'-reh*

flood, inondazione (f) *ee-non-dah-tsyoh'-neh*

floor, pavimento *pah-vee-men'-toh;* [storey], piano *pyah'-noh*

florist, fioraio *fyoh-rah'-yoh*

flower, fiore (m) *fyoh'-reh*

fluid, fluido, liquido *floo-ee'-doh, lee'-kwee-doh*

fly [insect], mosca *mos'-kah*

fly v., volare *voh-lah'-reh* [89]

fog, nebbia *nehb'-byah* [6]

follow, seguire *seh-gwee-reh*

food, cibo, vitto *chee'-boh, veet'-toh*

foot, piede (m) *pyeh'-deh*

for, per *per*

forbid, proibire, vietare *proh-ee-bee'-reh, vyeh-tah'-reh*

forbidden, proibito, vietato *proh-ee-bee'-toh, vyeh-tah'-toh*

forehead, fronte (f) *fron'-teh*

foreign, estero, straniero *es'-teh-roh, strah-nyeh'-roh*

foreigner, straniero, forestiere *strah-nyeh'-roh, foh-res-tyeh'-reh*

forest, selva, foresta *sel'-vah, foh-res'-tah*

forget, dimenticare *dee-men-tee-kah'-reh*

forgive, perdonare *per-doh-nah'-reh*

fork, forchetta *fohr-ket'-tah* [55]

form, forma *for'-mah*

former, precedente *preh-cheh-den'-teh*

formerly, prima *pree'-mah*

fort, forte (m) *for'-teh*

fortunate, fortunato *for-too-nah'-toh*

fortunately, fortunatamente *for-too-nah-tah-men'-tah*

forty, quaranta *kwah-rahn'-tah*

forward, avanti *ah-vahn'-tee*

fountain, fontana *fon-tah'-nah*

four, quattro *kwaht'-troh*

fourteen, quattordici *kwaht-tor'-dee-chee*

fourth, quarto *kwahr'-toh*

fracture n., frattura *fraht-too'-rah*

fragile, fragile *frah'-jee-leh*

free, libero *lee'-beh-roh* [44]

freedom, libertà *lee-ber-tah'*

freeze, gelare *jeh-lah'-reh*

frequently, frequentemente *freh-kwen-teh-men'-teh*

fresh, fresco *fres'-koh* [52]

Friday, venerdì *ve-ner-dee'*

fried, fritto *freet'-toh*

friend, amico *ah-mee'-koh,* [2]

friendly, amichevole *ah-mee-keh'-voh-leh*

from, da *dah*

front, fronte (f) *fron'-teh* **in front of,** davanti a *dah-vahn'-tee ah*

frozen, congelato *kon-jeh-lah'-toh*

fruit, frutta *froot'-tah* [52]

full, pieno *pyeh'-noh*
fun, divertimento *dee-ver-tee-men'-toh*
function, funzione (f) *foon-tsyoh'-neh*
funnel, imbuto *eem-boo'-toh*
funny, comico *koh'-mee-koh*
fur, pelo *peh'-loh*
furnished, ammobiliato *ahm-moh-bee-lee-yah'-toh*
furniture, mobili *moh'-bee-lee*
further, inoltre, di più *een-ol'-treh, dee pyoo*
future, futuro, avvenire (m) *foo-too'-roh, ahv-veh-nee'-reh*

gain *v.*, guadagnare *gwah-dahn-yah'-reh*
gamble *v.*, giocare *joh-kah'-reh*
game, gioco *joh'-koh*
gangplank, passerella, scalandrone (m) *pahs-seh-rehl'-lah, skah-lahn-droh'-neh* [88]
garage, autorimessa *ow-toh-ree-mes'-sah* [73, 76]
garden, giardino *jahr-dee'-noh*
garlic, aglio *ahl'-yoh*
gas, gas *gahs*
gasoline, benzina *ben-dzee'-nah* [73, 74]
gas station, stazione di servizio *stah-tsyoh'-neh dee ser-vee'-tsyoh* [73]
gate, cancello, porta *kahn-chel'-loh, por'-tah* [89]
gather [collect], raccogliere *rahk-kol'-yeh-reh*
gay, gaio *gah'-yoh*
general *adj.*, generale *jeh-neh-rah'-leh* **generally, in general**, generalmente *jeh-neh-rahl-men'-teh*
generous, generoso *jeh-neh-roh'-zoh*
gentleman, signore *seen-yoh'-reh*
get, ottenere *ot-teh-neh'-reh* **get in, get on**, salire *sah-lee'-reh* [46] **get off**, scendere *shen'-deh-reh* [46] **get up**, alzarsi *ah-tsahr'-see* [96]
gift, regalo *reh-gah'-loh*
gin, gin *jeen*

girl, ragazza *rah-gaht'-tsah* [10]

give, dare *dah'-reh* [13, 32]

glad, contento *kon-ten'-toh*

gladly, con piacere, volentieri *kon-pyah-cheh'-reh, voh-len-tyeh'-ree*

glass [for drinking], bicchiere *beek-kyeh'-reh* [51, 52, 55]

glasses [for the eyes], occhiali (m, pl) *ok-kyah'-lee*

glove, guanto *gwahn'-toh*

go, andare *ahn-dah'-reh* [12, 35, 44, 46, 88, 102] **go back,** tornare *tohr-nah'-reh* **go in,** entrare *en-trah'-reh* **go out,** uscire *oo-shee'-reh*

God, Dio *dee'-yoh*

gold, oro *oh'-roh*

good, buono *bwoh'-noh*

good-bye, arrivederci *ahr-ree-veh-der'-chee*

government, governo *goh-ver'-noh*

grandfather, nonno *non'-noh*

grandmother, nonna *non'-nah*

grape(s), uva *oo'-vah*

grapefruit, pompelmo *pom-pel'-moh*

grass, erba *er'-bah*

grateful, grato *grah'-toh*

gray, grigio *gree'-joh*

grease *n.,* grasso *grahs'-soh*

great, grande *grahn'-deh*

green, verde *ver'-deh*

grocery, bottega bi comestibili *bot-teh'-gah dee koh-mes-tee'-bee-lee*

ground, terra *ter'-rah*

group, gruppo *groop'-poh*

grow, crescere *kreh'-sheh-reh*

guard *n.,* guardia *gwahr'-dyah*

guest, ospite (m) *os'-pee-teh*

guide *n.,* guida *gwee'-dah* [99]

guilty, colpevole *kol-peh'-voh-leh*

guitar, chitarra *kee-tahr'-rah*

gum [chewing], gomma da masticare *gom'-mah dah mahs-tee-kah'-reh*

gun, fucile (m) *foo-chee'-leh*

habit, abitudine (f) *ah-bee-too'-dee-neh*

hair, capelli (m, pl) *keh-pel'-lee*

haircut, taglio di capelli *tahl'-yoh dee kah-pel'-lee*

hairdresser, parrucchiere (m) *pahr-rook-kyeh'-reh*

hairpin, forcella *for-chel'-lah*

half *adj.*, mezzo *med'-dzoh*

half *n.*, metà *meh-tah'*

hall, corridoio *kor-ree-doh'-yoh*

ham, proscuitto *proh-shoot'-toh*

hand, mano (f) *mah'-noh*

handkerchief, fazzoletto *faht-tsoh-let'-toh* [40]

hand-made, fatto a mano *faht'-toh ah mah'-noh*

handsome, bello *bel'-loh* [10]

hang, impiccare *eem-peek-kah'-reh*   **hang up**, appendere *ahp-pen-deh'-reh*

hanger [for clothing], attaccapanni *aht-tahk-kah-pahn'-nee*

happen, succedere *sooch-cheh'-deh-reh* [15]

happy, felice *feh-lee'-cheh*

harbor, porto *por'-toh* [86]

hard, duro *doo'-roh*

hardly, appena *ahp-peh'-nah*

harm *n.*, male (m) *mah'-leh*

harm *v.*, far male *fahr mah'-leh*

harmful, nocivo *noh-chee'-voh*

haste, fretta *fret'-tah*

hat, cappello *kahp-pel'-loh*

hat shop, cappelleria *kahp-pel-leh-ree'-yah*

hate *v.*, odiare *oh-dee-yah'-reh*

have, avere *ah-veh'-reh*   **I have**, ho *oh*   **have you?** ha Lei? *ah leh'-ee*

he, egli. lui *ehl'-yee, loo'-ee*

head, testa *tes'-tah*

headache, mal di testa *mahl dee tes'-tah* [92]

health, salute (f) *sah-loo'-teh* [56]

hear, udire, sentire *oo-dee'-reh, sen-tee'-reh*

heart, cuore (m) *kwoh'-reh*

heat *n.,* calore (m) *kah-loh'-reh*

heavy, pesante *peh-zahn'-teh*

heel, tacco *tahk'-koh*

hello, ciao, buon giorno *chow, bwon johr'-noh*

help *n.,* aiuto, soccorso *ah-yoo'-toh, sok-kor'-soh*

help *v.,* aiutare *ah-yoo-tah'-reh* [14, 64]

helpful, soccorrevole *sok-kor-reh'-voh-leh*

hem *n.,* orlo *ohr'-loh*

hen, gallina *gahl-lee'-nah*

her, la, lei *lah, leh'-ee*

here, qui, qua *kwee, kwah*

hers, suo, sua *soo'-oh, soo'-ah*

high, alto *ahl'-toh*

hill, collina *kol-lee'-nah*

him, lo, lui *loh, loo'-ee*

hip, anca *ahn'-kah*

hire, noleggiare *noh-lej-jah'-reh* [72]

his, suo, sua *soo'-oh, soo'-ah*

history, storia *stoh'-ree-yah*

hit *v.,* colpire *kol-pee'-reh*

hold, tenere *teh-neh'-reh*

hole, buco *boo'-koh*

holiday, giorno festivo, giorno di festa *johr'-noh fes-tee'-voh, johr'-noh dee fes'-tah*

holy, santo *sahn'-toh*

home, casa *kah'-zah*

honest, onesto *oh-nes'-toh*

honey [food], miele (m) *myeh'-leh*

honor, onore (m) *oh-noh'-reh*

hope *n.,* speranza *speh-rahn'-tsah*

hope *v.,* sperare *speh-rah'-reh* [3]

horn [automobile], tromba *trom'-bah*
hors d'oeuvres, antipasto *ahn-tee-pahs'-toh*
horse, cavallo *kah-vahl'-loh*
hospital, ospedale (m) *os-peh-dah'-leh* [92]
host, oste (m) *os'-teh*
hot, caldo *kahl'-doh*
hotel, albergo *ahl-ber'-goh* [10, 32, 36, 38, 45, 53, 70, 102]
hour, ora *oh'-rah*
house, casa *kah'-zah*
how, come *ko'-meh* **how are you?** come sta? *ko'-meh
    stah* **how far?** quanto lontano? *kwahn'-toh lon-tah'-
    noh* **how long?** quanto tempo? *kwahn'-toh tem'-poh*
    how many? quanti? quante? *kwahn'-tee, kwahn'-teh*
    how much? quanto? *kwahn'-toh*
hug *n.,* abbraccio *ahb-brahch'-choh*
human, umano *oo-mah'-noh*
humid, umido *oo'-mee-doh*
hundred, cento *chen'-toh*
hunger, fame (f) *fah'-meh*
hungry: to be hungry, aver fame *ah-vehr' fah'-meh* [47, 48]
hurry *v.,* affrettarsi *ahf-fret-tahr'-see* **to be in a hurry,**
    aver fretta *ah-vehr' fret'-tah*
hurt, far male *fahr mah'-leh* [93]
husband, marito *mah-ree'-toh* [2]

I, io *ee'-yoh*
ice, ghiaccio *gyahch'-choh* [55]
ice cream, gelato *jeh-lah'-toh* [56]
idea, idea *ee-deh'-yah*
identification, identificazione (f) *ee-den-tee-fee-kah-tsyoh'-
    neh*
if, se *seh*
ill, ammalato *ahm-mah-lah'-toh*
illegal, illegale *eel-leh-gah'-leh*
illness, malattia *mah-laht-tee'-yah*

imagine, immaginare, figurarsi *eem-mah-jee-nah'-reh, fee-goo-rahr'-see*

immediately, immediatamente, subito *eem-meh-dee-yah-tah-men'-teh, soo'-bee-toh*

important, importante *eem-por-tahn'-teh*

impossible, impossibile *eem-pos-see'-bee-leh* [13]

improve, migliorare *meel-yoh-rah'-reh*

improvement, miglioramento *meel-yoh-rah-men'-toh*

in, in *een*

incident, incidente (m) *een-chee-den'-teh*

included, incluso, compreso *een-kloo'-zoh, kom-preh'-zoh* [57]

incomplete, incompleto *een-kom-pleh'-toh*

inconvenient, inconveniente *een-kon-veh-nyen'-teh*

incorrect, inesatto *een-eh-zaht'-toh*

increase *v.,* aumentare *ow-men-tah'-reh*

incredible, incredibile *een-kreh-dee'-bee-leh*

indeed, in verità *een veh-ree-tah'*

independence, indipendenza *een-dee-pen-den'-tsah*

independent, indipendente *een-dee-pen-den'-teh*

indicate, indicare *een-dee-kah'-reh*

indigestion, indigestione (f) *een-dee-jes-tyoh'-neh*

indoors, dentro *den'-troh*

industrial, industriale *een-doos-tree-yah'-leh*

inexpensive, a buon mercato *ah bwon mehr-kah'-toh*

infection, infezione (f) *een-feh-tsyoh'-neh*

infectious, infettivo *een-fet-tee'-voh*

inform, informare *een-fohr-mah'-reh*

information, informazioni (f, pl) *een-fohr-mah-tsyoh'-nee*

injection, iniezione (f) *een-yeh-tsyoh'-neh*

injury, ferita, danno, lesione (f) *feh-ree'-tah, dahn'-noh, leh-zyoh'-neh*

injustice, ingiustizia *een-joos-tee'-tsyah*

ink, inchiostro *een-kyohs'-troh*

inn, taverna *tah-ver'-nah*

inquire, domandare, informarsi *doh-mahn-dah'-reh, een-fohr-mahr'-see*

inside, dentro *den'-troh*

insist, insistere *een-sees'-teh-reh*

inspect, ispezionare *ee-speh-tsee-yoh-nah'-reh*

instead of, invece di *een-veh'-cheh dee*

institution, istituzione (f) *ee-stee-toot-syoh'-neh*

insurance, assicurazione (f) *ahs-see-koo-rah-tsyoh'-neh*

insure, assicurare *ahs-see-koo-rah'-reh*

intelligent, intelligente *een-tel-lee-jen'-teh*

intend, intendere *een-ten'-deh-reh*

intense, intenso *een-ten'-soh*

intention, intenzione (f) *een-ten-tsyoh'-neh*

interest *n.,* interesse (m) *een-teh-res'-seh*

interest *v.,* interessare *een-teh-res-sah'-reh*

interesting, interessante *een-teh-res-sahn'-teh* [102]

intermission, intervallo *een-ter-vahl-loh*

internal, interno *een-ter'-noh*

international, internazionale *een-ter-nah-tsee-yoh-nah'-leh*

interpret, interpretare *een-ter-preh-tah'-reh*

interpreter, interprete (m) *een-ter'-preh-teh*

interview *n.,* intervista *een-ter-vees'-tah*

into, in *een*

introduce, presentare *preh-zen-tah'-reh*

introduction, presentazione (f) *preh-zen-tah-tsyoh'-neh*

investigate, investigare *een-ves-tee-gah'-reh*

invitation, invito *een-vee'-toh*

invite, invitare *een-vee-tah'-reh*

iron [for ironing], ferro da stiro *fer'-roh dah stee'-roh*

iron [metal], ferro *fer'-roh*

iron *v.,* stirare *stee-rah'-reh*

is: è, sta *eh, stah* **he is,** lui è *loo'-ee eh* **she is,** lei è *leh'-ee eh* **it is,** è *eh*

island, isola *ee'-zoh-lah*

itch *v.,* prudere *proo'-deh-reh*

jacket, giacca *jahk'-kah* [8]
jail, carcere (m) *kahr'-cheh-reh*
jam, confettura *kon-fet-too'-rah*
January, gennaio *jen-nah'-yoh*
jaw, mandibola *mahn-dee'-boh-lah*
jelly, gelatina *jeh-lah-tee'-nah*
jewelry, gioielli (m, pl) *joh-yel'-lee*
jewelry store, gioielleria *joh-yel-leh-ree'-yah*
job, compito, lavoro *kom'-pee-toh, lah-voh'-roh*
joke, scherzo *sker'-tsoh*
juice, succo *sook'-koh*
July, luglio *lool'-yoh*
jump *v.*, saltare *sahl-tah'-reh*
June, giugno *joon'-yoh*
just, giusto *joos'-toh*
justice, giustizia *joos-tee'-tsee-yah*

keep, mantenere *mahn-teh-neh'-reh*
key, chiave (f) *kyah'-veh* [34, 39, 73, 87]
kidneys, reni *reh'-nee*
kill, uccidere, ammazzare *och-chee'-deh-reh, ahm-mahd-dzah'-reh*
kilogram, chilogrammo *kee-loh-grahm'-moh*
kilometer, chilometro *kee-loh'-me-troh* [72]
kind *adj.*, gentile *jen-tee'-leh*
kind *n.*, specie (f) *speh'-chyeh* [31]
king, re *reh*
kiss *n.*, bacio *bah'-choh*
kiss *v.*, baciare *bah-chah'-reh*
kitchen, cucina *koo-chee'-nah*
knee, ginocchio *jee-nok'-kyoh*
knife, coltello *kol-tel'-loh* [55]
knock *v.*, bussare *boos-sah'-reh*
know [something], sapere *sah-peh'-reh* [9]; [someone], conoscere *koh-noh'-sheh-reh* [10]

laborer, lavoratore (m), operaio *lah-voh-rah-toh'-reh, oh-peh-rah'-yoh*

lace, merletto *mer-let'-toh*

ladies' room, gabinetto da signore *gah-bee-net'-toh dah seen-yoh'-reh*

lady, signora *seen-yoh'-rah*

lake, lago *lah'-goh*

lamb, agnello *an-yel'-loh*

lame, zoppo *dzop'-poh*

lamp, lampada *lahm'-pah-dah*

land *n.*, terra *ter'-rah*

land *v.*, atterrare *aht-ter-rah'-reh* [90]

landing card, cartoncino (permesso) di sbarco *kahr-ton-chee'-noh (per-mes'-soh) dee zbahr'-koh* [88]

language, lingua *leen'-gwah*

large, grande, grosso *grahn'-deh, gros'-soh*

last *adj.*, ultimo *ool'-tee-moh*

last *v.*, durare *doo-rah'-reh* [99]

late, tardi *tahr'-dee* [24, 84]

laugh *v.*, ridere *ree'-deh-reh*

laughter, riso *ree'-zoh*

laundry, lavanderia *lah-vahn-deh-ree'-yah*

lavatory, gabinetto *gah-bee-net'-toh* [85]

law, legge (f) *lej-jeh*

lawyer, avvocato *ahv-voh-kah'-toh*

lazy, pigro *peeg'-roh*

lead *v.*, condurre *kon-door'-reh*

leaf, foglia *fohl'-yah*

leak *n.*, perdita *per'-dee-tah*

learn, imparare *eem-pah-rah'-reh*

least, minimo *mee'-nee-moh*

leather, cuoio *kwoh'-yoh*

leave, partire, andarsene *pahr-tee'-reh, ahn-dahr'-seh-neh* [25, 40, 46, 83, 85, 88]

left, sinistro *see-nees'-troh* [45]

leg, gamba *gahm'-bah* [93]

lemon, limone (m) *lee-moh'-neh*

lend, prestare *pres-tah'-reh*

length, lunghezza *loon-get'-tsah*

lens, lente (f) *len'-teh*   **contact lens,** lente (f) *len'-teh*

less, meno *meh'-noh*

let, lasciare *lah-shah'-reh*

letter, lettera *let'-teh-rah* [40]

lettuce, lattuga *laht-too'-gah*

liberty, libertà *lee-ber-tah'*

library, biblioteca *bee-blee-oh-teh'-kah*

license, licenza, patente (f) *lee-chen'-tsah, pah-ten'-teh* [76]

lie [untruth], bugia, menzogna *boo-jee'-yah, men-tsohn'-yah*

lie: to lie down, coricarsi *koh-ree-kahr'-see* [96]

life, vita *vee'-tah*

lift *v.,* sollevare *sol-leh-vah'-reh*

light [weight], leggero *lej-jeh'-roh*; [color], chiaro *kyah'-roh*

light *n.,* luce (f) *loo'-cheh*

lighter [cigarette], accendi-sigari (m) *ahch-chen'-dee see'-gah-ree*

lightning, lampo, fulmine (m) *lahm'-poh, fool'-mee-neh* [00]

like *adv.,* come *ko'-meh*

like *v.,* piacere a *pyah-cheh'-reh* *ah* [7, 36, 67, 102]   **I would like,** vorrei *vor-reh'-ee* [37, 52, 69, 98]

line, linea *lee'-neh-ah*

linen, lino *lee'-noh*

lip, labbro *lahb'-broh*

lipstick, matita per le labbra *mah-tee'-tah per leh lahb'-brah*

liqueur, liquore (m) *lee-kwoh'-reh*

list, lista *lees'-tah*

listen, ascoltare *ahs-kol-tah'-reh*

liter, litro *leet'-roh* [74]

little, piccolo *peek'-koh-loh* **a little,** un poco *oon poh'-koh* [11]

live *v.*, vivere, abitare *vee'-veh-reh, ah-bee-tah'-reh* [10]

liver, fegato *feh'-gah-toh*

lobby, atrio *ah'-tree-yoh*

lobster, aragosta *ah-rah-gos'-tah*

long, lungo *loon'-goh* [68, 69]

look *v.*, guardare *gwahr-dah'-reh*

loose, sciolto *shol'-toh* [69]

lose, perdere *per'-deh-reh* [16, 39]

lost, perduto *per-doo'-toh*

lot: a lot of, molto *mol'-toh*

lotion, lozione (f) *loh-tsyoh'-neh*

loud, ad alta voce *ahd ahl'-tah voh'-cheh*

love *n.*, amore (m) *ah-moh'-reh*

love *v.*, amare *ah-mah'-reh* [10]

low, basso *bahs'-soh*

lubricate *v.*, lubricare *loo-bree-kah'-reh*

luck, fortuna *for-too'-nah* **good luck,** buona fortuna *bwoh'-nah for-too'-nah*

lucky, fortunato *for-too-nah'-toh* **to be lucky,** essere fortunato *es'-seh-reh for-too-nah'-toh*

luggage, bagaglio *bah-gahl'-yoh* [35, 40, 44, 48]

lunch, seconda colazione *seh-kon'-dah koh-lah-tsyoh'-neh* [48]

lung, polmone (m) *pol-moh'-neh*

machine, macchina *mahk'-kee-nah*

madam, signora *seen-yoh'-rah*

magazine, rivista *ree-vees'-tah*

mail *n.*, posta *pos'-tah* [32]

mailbox, buca da lettere, cassetta postale *boo'-kah dah let'-teh-reh, kahs-set'-tah pos-tah'-leh*

main, principale *preen-chee-pah'-leh* **main course,** piatto principale *pyaht'-toh preen-chee-pah'-leh*

major, maggiore *mahj-joh'-reh*

make, fare *fah'-reh*

male, maschio, maschile (m) *mahs'-kyoh, mahs-kee'-leh*

man, uomo *woh'-moh* [10, 15]

manager, gerente (m), *direttore* (m) *jeh-ren'-teh, dee-ret-toh'-reh*

manicure, manicure (f) *mah-nee-koo'-reh*

manner, maniera *mah-nyeh'-rah*

manufactured, fabbricato *fahb-bree-kah'-toh*

many, molti, molte *mol'-tee, mol'-teh*

map, carta geografica *kahr'-tah jeh-oh-grah'-fee-kah* [75]

marble, marmo *mahr'-moh*

March, marzo *mahr'-tsoh*

mark, marca *mahr'-kah*

market, mercato *mer'-kah-toh*

marketplace, mercato *mer-kah'-toh*

marmalade, marmellata *mahr-mel-lah'-tah*

married, sposato *spoh-zah'-toh*

marry, sposarsi *spoh-zahr'-see*

marvelous, meraviglioso *meh-rah-veel-yoh'-zoh*

mass [church], messa *mes'-sah*

massage *n.,* massaggio *mahs-sahj'-joh*

match, fiammifero *fyahm-mee'-feh-roh* [70]

material, materiale (m) *mah-teh-ree-yah'-leh*

matter: no matter, non importa *non eem-por'-tah* **what is the matter?** che c'è? *keh cheh*

May, maggio *mahj'-joh*

may, potere *poh-teh'-reh* **I may,** posso *pos'-soh* **may I?** posso? *pos'-soh*

maybe, forse *for'-seh*

me, me, mi *meh, mee* **to me,** mi, me *mee, meh*

meal, pasto *pahs'-toh* [38, 48, 53, 90]

mean *v.,* significare, voler dire *seen-yee-fee-kah'-reh, voh-lehr' dee'-reh* [12]

measure *n.,* misura *mee-zoo'-rah*

measure *v.,* misurare *mee-zoo-rah'-reh*

meat, carne (f) *kahr'-neh* [56]

mechanic, meccanico *mek-kah'-nee-koh* [74]

medicine, medicina *meh-dee-chee'-nah* [96]

medium, medio *meh'-dyoh*

meet, incontrare *een-kon-trah'-reh* [3]

melon, melone (m) *meh-loh'-neh*

member, membro *mem'-broh*

memory, memoria *meh-moh'-ree-yah*

mend, rammendare *rahm-men-dah'-reh*

men's room, gabinetto per signori *gah-bee-net'-toh per seen-yoh'-ree*

mention *v.*, menzionare *men-tsee-yoh-nah'-reh*

menu, lista *lees'-tah* [50]

message, messaggio *mes-sahj-joh*

messenger, messaggero *mes-sahj-jeh'-roh*

metal, metallo *meh-tahl'-loh*

meter [measure], metro *meh'-troh*

middle, mezzo *med'-dzoh·*

midnight, mezzanotte *med-dzah-not'-teh* [24]

mild, mite *mee'-teh*

milk, latte (m) *laht'-teh* [52, 53]

milliner, modista *moh-dees'-tah*

million, milione *meel-yoh'-neh*

mind, mente (f) *men'-teh*

mine, mio *mee'-yoh*

mineral, minerale *mee-neh-rah'-leh*

mineral water, acqua minerale *ahk'-kwah mee-neh-rah'-leh*

minute, minuto *mee-noo'-toh*

mirror, specchio *spek'-kyoh* [73]

misfortune, disgrazia *dees-grah'-tsee-yah*

Miss, signorina *seen-yoh-ree'-nah*

missing, manca, mancante *mahn'-kah, mahn-kahn'-teh*

mistake *n.*, sbaglio *zbahl'-yoh* [57]

mistaken, sbagliato *zbah-lyah'-toh*

mix *v.*, mescolare *mes-koh-lah'-reh*

mixed, mescolato, misto *mes-koh-lah'-toh, mees'-toh*

model, modello *moh-del'-loh*

modern, moderno *moh-der'-noh*

modest, modesto *moh-des'-toh*

moment, momento *moh-men'-toh*

Monday, lunedì *loo-neh-dee'*

money, denaro *deh-nah'-roh* [15, 31, 32]

money order, vaglia *vahl'-yah*

monk, monaco *moh'-nah-koh*

month, mese (m) *meh'-zeh* **per month, a month,** al mese *ahl meh'-zeh*

monument, monumento *moh-noo-men'-toh* [101]

moon, luna *loo'-nah* [7]

more, più *pyoo*

morning, mattina, mattino *maht-tee'-nah, maht-tee'-noh* [100] **good morning,** buon giorno *bwon johr'-noh*

mosquito, zanzara *dzahn-dzah'-rah*

mosquito net, zanzariera *dzahn-dzah-ree-yeh'-rah*

most, il più (m), la più (f) *eel pyoo, lah pyoo* **most of,** la maggior parte di, la maggioranza di *lah mahj-johr' pahr'-teh dee, lah mahj-joh-rahn'-tsah dee*

mother, madre *mah'-dreh* [3]

motion, mozione (f), moto, movimento *moh-tsyoh'-neh, moh'-toh, moh-vee-men'-toh*

motor, motore (m) *moh-toh'-reh*

mountain, montagna *mon-tahn'-yah*

mouth, bocca *bok'-kah*

move *v.,* muovere, trasferire *mwoh'-veh-reh, trahs-feh-ree'-reh* [16]

movie, cinema (m) *chee'-neh-mah* [101]

Mr., signore *seen-yoh'-reh*

Mrs., signora *seen-yoh'-rah*

much, molto, molta *mol'-toh, mol-tah* **very much,** moltissimo *mol-tees'-see-moh* **too much,** troppo *trop'-poh* **how much?** quanto? *kwahn'-toh*

mud, fango *fahn'-goh*

muffler, silenziatore (m) *see-len-tsee-yah-toh'-reh*
muscle, muscolo *moos'-koh-loh*
museum, museo *moo-zeh'-oh* [46, 99]
mushroom, fungo *foon'-goh*
music, musica *moo'-zee-kah*
musician, musicista *moo-zee-chees'-tah*
must, dovere *doh-veh'-reh*   **I must,** devo *deh'-voh*
mustache, baffi (pl) *bahf'-fee*
mustard, mostarda, senape (m) *mos-tahr'-dah, seh'-nah-peh*
mutton, montone (m) *mon-toh'-neh*
my, mio *mee'-yoh*
myself, io stesso *ee'-yoh stes'-soh*

nail [fingernail], unghia *oon'-gyah*
nailfile, lima da unghie *lee'-mah dah oon'-gyeh*
naked, nudo *noo'-doh*
name, nome (m) *noh'-meh* [9, 10]   **last name,** cognome (m) *kon-yoh'-meh*   **what is your name?** come si chiama Lei? *ko'-meh see kyah'-mah leh'-se*   **my name is . . . ,** mi chiamo . . . *mee kyah'-moh . . .*
napkin, tovagliolo *toh-vahl-yoh'-loh* [55]
narrow, stretto *stret'-toh* [69, 75]
nation, nazione (f) *nah-tsyoh'-neh*
national, nazionale *nah-tsyoh-nah'-leh*
nationality, nazionalità *nah-tsyoh-nah-lee-tah'*
native, nativo *nah-tee'-voh*
natural, naturale *nah-too-rah'-leh*
naturally, naturalmente *nah-too-rahl-men'-teh*
nature, natura *nah-too'-rah*
near, vicino *vee-chee'-noh*
nearly, circa, quasi *cheer'-kah, kwah'-zee*
necessary, necessario *neh-chehs-sah'-ree-yoh*
neck, collo *kol'-loh*
necklace, collana *kol-lah'-nah*
necktie, cravatta *krah-vaht'-tah*

need *v.*, aver bisogno di *ah-vehr' bee-zon'-yoh dee*
  I need, ho bisogno di, mi occorre *oh bee-zon'-yoh dee,*
  mee ok-kor'-reh
needle, ago *ah'-goh* [70]
neighbor, vicino *vee-chee'-noh*
neighborhood, vicinato *vee-chee-nah'-toh*
neither . . . nor . . . , nè . . . nè . . . *neh . . . neh . . .*
nephew, nipote (m) *nee-poh'-teh*
nerve, nervo *ner'-voh*
nervous, nervoso *ner-voh'-zoh*
never, mai, non . . . mai . . . *mah'-ee, non . . . mah'-ee*
nevertheless, tuttavia *toot-tah-vee'-yah*
new, nuovo *nwoh'-voh*
news, notizia, notizie *noh-tee'-tsyah, noh-tee'-tsyeh*
newspaper, giornale (m) *johr-nah'-leh*
next *adj.*, prossimo *pros'-see-moh*
next, *adv.*, quindi *kween'-dee* [85]
nice, simpatico *seem-pah'-tee-koh*
niece, nipote (f) *nee-poh'-teh*
night, notte (f) *not'-teh* **good night,** buona notte *bwoh'-*
  nah not'-teh
nightclub, locale notturno (m) *loh-kah'-leh not-toor'-noh*
nightgown, camicia da notte *kah-mee'-chah dah not'-teh*
nine, nove *noh'-veh*
nineteen, diciannove *dee-chahn-noh'-veh*
ninety, novanta *noh-vahn'-tah*
ninth, nono *noh'-noh*
no, no *noh*
noise, rumore (m) *roo-moh'-reh*
noisy, rumoroso *roo-moh-roh'-zoh*
none, nessuno *nes-soo'-noh*
noodles, taglierini (m,pl), fettuccine (f, pl) *tahl-yeh-ree'-*
  nee, fet-tooch-chee'-neh
noon, mezzogiorno *med-dzoh-johr'-noh* [24]
no one, nessuno *nes-soo'-noh*
north, nord (m) *nord*

northeast, nord-est *nord-est'*
northwest, nord-ovest *nord-oh'-vest*
nose, naso *nah'-zoh*
not, non *non*
notebook, quaderno *kwah-dehr'-noh*
nothing, niente *nyen'-teh* **nothing else**, nient'altro *nyent-ahl'-troh*
notice *n.*, avviso *ahv-vee'-zoh*
notice *v.*, notare *noh-tah'-reh*
notify, notificare *noh-tee-fee-kah'-reh*
novel [book], romanzo *roh-mahn'-dzoh*
November, novembre *noh-vem'-breh*
novocaine, novocaina *noh-voh-kah-ee'-nah*
now, adesso, ora *ah-des'-soh, oh'-rah*
nowhere, in nessun luogo *een nes-soon' lwoh'-goh*
number, numero *noo'-meh-roh* [39, 42, 88]
nun, monaca *moh'-nah-kah*
nurse, infermiera *een-fer-myeh'-rah*
nursemaid, governante (f) *goh-ver-nahn'-teh*
nut, nuts, noce, noci (f) *noh'-cheh, noh'-chee*

obey, obbedire *ob-beh-dee'-reh*
obliged, obbligato *ohb-blee-gah'-toh*
obtain, ottenere *ot-teh-neh'-reh*
obvious, ovvio *ov'-vyoh*
occasionally, occasionalmente, di tempo in tempo *ok-kah-zyoh-nahl-men'-teh, dee tem'-poh een tem'-poh*
occupation, occupazione (f) *ok-koo-pah-tsyoh'-neh*
occupied, occupato *ok-koo-pah'-toh* [86]
ocean, oceano *oh-cheh'-ah-noh* [37]
October, ottobre *ot-toh'-breh*
odd [unusual], raro *rah'-roh*
odd [number], dispari *dees'-pah-ree*
of, di *dee*
offer *v.*, offrire *of-free'-reh*
office, ufficio *oof-fee'-choh*

official *adj.*, ufficiale *oof-fee-chah'-leh*

often, spesso *spes'-soh*

oil, olio *oh'-lyoh* [74]

old, vecchio, anziano *vek'-kyoh*, *ahn-tsyah'-noh*

olive, oliva *oh-lee'-vah*

omelet, frittata, omeletta *freet-tah'-tah*, *oh-meh-let'-tah*

on, su *soo*

once, una volta *oo'-nah vol'-tah*

one, uno, un, una, un' *oo'-noh*, *oon*, *oo'-nah*, *oon*

one-way [street], senso unico *sen'-soh oo'-nee-koh*; [ticket], solo andata *soh'-loh ahn-dah'-tah* [84]

onion, cipolla *chee-pol'-lah*

only, soltanto, solamente *sol-tahn'-toh*, *soh-lah-men'-teh*

open *adj.*, aperto *ah-per'-toh* [100]

open *v.*, aprire *ah-pree'-reh* [34, 39, 62, 84, 99, 100]

opera, opera *oh'-peh-rah*

operation, operazione (f) *oh-peh-rah-tsyoh'-neh*

operator [telephone], telefonista, centralino *teh-leh-foh-nees'-tah*, *chen-trah-lee'-noh*

opinion, opinione (f) *oh-pee-nyoh'-neh*

opportunity, occasione, opportunità (f) *ok-kah-zyoh'-neh*, *oppor-too-nee-tah'*

opposite, opposto *op-pos'-toh*

optician, ottico *ot'-tee-koh*

or, o, od *oh*, *ohd*

orange, arancia *ah-rahn'-chah*

order *v.*, ordinare *or-dee-nah'-reh* [56]   **in order to**, per *per*

ordinary, ordinario *or-dee-nah'-ree-yoh*

oriental, orientale *oh-ree-en-tah'-leh*

original, originale *oh-ree-jee-nah'-leh*

ornament, ornamento *or-nah-men'-toh*

other, altro *ahl'-troh*

ought, dovere *doh-veh'-reh*

our, ours, nostro, il nostro *nos'-troh*, *eel nos'-troh*

out *adv.*, fuori *fwoh'-ree*

outdoor, all'aperto *ahl-lah-per'-toh*

out of order, non funziona *non foon-tsyoh'-nah*

outside *adv.*, fuori *fwoh'-ree*   **outside of,** fuori di *fwoh'-ree dee*

over [ended] *adj.*, finito *fee-nee'-toh*

over [above] *prep.*, sopra *so'-prah*

overcharge *n.*, prezzo eccessivo *pret'-tsoh ech-ches-see'-voh*

overcoat, soprabito *so-prah'-bee-toh*

overcooked, troppo cotto *trop'-poh kot'-toh*

overhead, in alto, di sopra *een ahl'-toh, dee so'-prah*

overturn, capovolgere *kah-poh-vol'-jeh-reh*

owe, dovere *doh-veh'-reh* [56]

own *adj.*, proprio *proh'-pree-yoh*

owner, proprietario *proh-pree-yeh-tah'-ree-yoh*

oyster, ostrica *os'-tree-kah*

pack *v.*, impaccare *eem-pahk-kah'-reh* [70]

package, pacco *pahk'-koh*

page, pagina *pah'-jee-nah*

paid, pagato *pah-gah'-toh*

pain, dolore (m) *doh-loh'-reh*

paint, pittura *peet-too'-rah*

paint *v.*, dipingere *dee-peen'-jeh-reh*

painting, pittura *peet-too'-rah*

pair, paio *pah'-yoh* [69]

palace, palazzo *pah-laht'-tsoh* [101]

pale, pallido *pahl'-lee-doh*

palm, palmo *pahl'-moh*

pants, pantaloni (m, pl) *pahn-tah-loh'-nee*

paper, carta *kahr'-tah*

parcel, pacco *pahk'-koh*

pardon, scusa *skoo'-zah*   **pardon me,** mi scusi *mee skoo'-zee*

parents, genitori *jeh-nee-toh'-ree*

park, parco *pahr'-koh* [101]

park [a car] *v.*, posteggiare, parcheggiare *pos-tej-jah'-reh,
   pahr-kej-jah'-reh* [76]
parsley, prezzemolo *pred-dzeh'-moh-loh*
part, parte (f) *pahr'-teh*
part [leave], partire *pahr-tee'-reh*
particular, particolare *pahr-tee-koh-lah'-reh*
partner [business], socio, *soh'-choh*
party, festa *fes'-tah*
pass *v.*, passare *pahs-sah'-reh*
passage, passaggio *pahs-sahj'-joh*
passenger, passeggero *pahs-sej-jeh'-roh*
passport, passaporto *pahs-sah-por'-toh* [16, 31, 33, 34]
past *adj. & n.*, passato *pahs-sah'-toh*
pastry, pasticceria *pahs-teech-cheh-ree'-yah*
path, sentiero *sen-tyeh'-roh*
patient *adj. & n.*, paziente *pah-tsyen'-teh*
pay *v.*, pagare *pah-gah'-reh* [34 ,57, 75] **to pay cash,**
   pagare in contante *pah-gah'-reh een kon-tahn'-teh* [70]
payment, pagamento *pah-gah-men'-toh*
pea, pisello *pee-zel'-loh*
peace, pace (f) *pah'-cheh*
peaceful, pacifico *pah-chee'-fee-koh*
peach, pesca *pes'-kah*
peak, picco *peek'-koh*
peanut, arachide (f) *ah-rah'-kee-deh*
pear, pera *peh'-rah*
pearl, perla *per'-lah*
peasant, contadino *kon-tah-dee'-noh*
peculiar, strano *strah'-noh*
pen, penna *pen'-nah* **fountain pen**, penna stilografica
   pen'-nah stee-loh-grah'-fee-kah
penalty, pena *peh'-nah*
pencil, matita *mah-tee'-tah*
penny, centesimo *chen-teh'-zee-moh*
people, gente (f) *jen'-teh*
pepper [spice], pepe (m) *peh'-peh*

peppermint, menta *men'-tah*
per, al, alla *ahl, ahl'-lah*
perfect, perfetto *per-fet'-toh*
performance, rappresentazione (f) *rahp-preh-zen-tah-tsyoh'-neh*
perfume, profumo *proh-foo'-moh*
perfumery, profumeria *proh-foo-meh-ree'-yah*
perhaps, forse *for'-seh*
period, periodo *peh-ree'-oh-doh*
permanent, permanente *per-mah-nen'-teh*
permission, permesso *per-mes'-soh*
permit *v.*, permettere *per-met'-teh-reh*
person, persona *per-soh'-nah*
personal, personale *per-soh-nah'-leh* [34]
perspiration, sudore (m) *soo-doh'-reh*
petrol, petrolio *peh-trohl'-yoh*
petticoat, sottoveste (f) *sot-toh-ves'-teh*
pharmacist, farmacista (m) *fahr-mah-chees'-tah*
pharmacy, farmacia *fahr-mah-chee'-yah*
photograph, fotografia *foh-toh-grah-fee'-yah*
photographer, fotografo *foh-toh'-grah-foh*
photography, fotografia *foh-toh-grah-fee'-yah*
photography shop, negozio di fotografia *neh-goh'-tsyoh dee foh-toh-grah-fee'-yah*
piano, pianoforte (m) *pee-yah-noh-for'-teh*
pick up, cogliere *kohl'-yeh-reh*
picture, quadro *kwah'-droh*
pie, torta *tor'-tah*
piece, pezzo *pet'-tsoh*
pier, molo *moh'-loh* [86]
pig, maiale, porco *mah-yah'-leh, por'-koh*
pigeon, piccione (m) *peech-choh'-neh*
pile, catasta, mucchio *kah-tahs'-tah, mook'-kyoh*
pill, pillola *peel'-loh-lah*
pillar, pilastro *pee-lahs'-troh*
pillow, guanciale (m) *gwahn-chah'-leh* [89]

pilot, pilota (m) *pee-loh'-tah*

pin, spillo *speel'-loh* [70]   **safety pin,** spillo di sicurezza *speel'-loh dee see-koo-ret'-tsah*

pineapple, ananasso *ah-nah-nahs'-soh*

pink, rosa *roh'-zah*

pipe [tobacco], pipa *pee'-pah*

place *n.*, posto, luogo *pos'-toh, lwoh'-goh* [99]

place *v.*, mettere, collocare *met'-teh-reh, kol-loh-kah'-reh*

plain [simple], semplice *sem'-plee-cheh*

plan *n.*, piano *pyah'-noh*

plant, pianta *pyahn'-tah*

plastic, plastico *plahs'-tee-koh*

plate, piatto *pyaht'-toh*

platform, piattaforma *pyaht-tah-for'-mah* [83]

play *v.*, giocare *joh-kah'-reh*

pleasant, piacevole *pyah-cheh'-voh-leh*

please [suit or satisfy], piacere a *pyah-cheh'-reh ah*   **if you please,** per favore, per piacere *per fah-voh'-reh, per pyah-cheh'-reh*

pleasure, piacere (m) *pyah-cheh'-reh* [4]

plenty of, molto, molti *mol'-toh, mol'-tee*

plum, susina *soo-zee'-nah*

pneumonia, polmonite (f) *pohl-moh-nee'-teh*

poached, cotto in camicia *kot'-toh een kah-mee'-chah*

pocket, tasca *tahs'-kah*

pocketbook [wallet], portafoglio *por-tah-fohl'-yoh*; [purse], borsa *bor'-sah*

point *n.*, punto *poon'-toh*

poison, veleno *veh-leh'-noh*

poisonous, velenoso *veh-leh-noh'-zoh*

police, polizia (f) *poh-lee-tsee'-yah* [15]

policeman, poliziotto, carabiniere (m) *poh-lee-tsee-yot'-toh, kah-rah-bee-nyeh'-reh*

police station, questura *kwes-too'-rah*

political, politico *poh-lee'-tee-koh*

pond, stagno *stahn'-yoh*

pool, piscina *pee-shee'-nah*
poor, povero *poh'-veh-roh*
popular, popolare *poh-poh-lah'-reh*
pork, carne di maiale (f) *kahr'-neh dee mah-yah'-leh*
port, porto *por'-toh* [86]
porter, facchino *fahk-kee'-noh* [35, 82, 83]
portrait, ritratto *ree-traht'-toh*
position, posizione (f) *poh-zee-tsyoh'-neh*
positive, positivo *poh-zee-tee'-voh*
possible, possibile *pos-see'-bee-leh* [13]
possibly, possibilmente *pos-see-beel-men'-teh*
postage, affrancatura *ahf-frahn-kah-too'-rah*
postage stamp, francobollo *frahn-koh-bol'-loh* [40]
postcard, cartolina postale *kahr-toh-lee'-nah pos-tah'-leh*
post office, ufficio postale *oof-fee'-choh pos-tah'-leh*
potato, patata *pah-tah'-tah*
pound [money], libbra *leeb'-brah* [31]
powder, cipria *cheep'-ree-yah*
power, potenza *poh-ten'-tsah*
powerful, potente *poh-ten'-teh*
practical, pratico *prah'-tee-koh*
practice *n.*, pratica *prah'-tee-kah*
prayer, preghiera *preh-gyeh'-rah*
precious, prezioso *preh-tsyoh'-zoh*
prefer, preferire *preh-feh-ree'reh*
preferable, preferibile *preh-feh-ree'-bee-leh*
pregnant, incinta *een-cheen'-tah*
premier, primo ministro *pree'-moh mee-nees'-troh*
preparation, preparazione (f) *preh-pah-rah-tsyoh'-neh*
prepare, preparare *preh-pah-rah'-reh*
prepay, pagare anticipatamente *pah-gah'-reh ahn-tee-chee-pah-tah-men'-teh*
prescription, prescrizione (f) *preh-skree-tsyoh'-neh* [96]
present [gift], regalo *reh-gah'-loh*; [time], attuale *aht-too-ah'-leh*
present *v.*, regalare *reh-gah-lah'-reh* [2]

press [clothes] *v.*, stirare *stee-rah'-reh*
pressure, pressione (f) *pres-syoh'-neh*
pretty, bello, grazioso *bel'-loh, grah-tsyoh'-zoh* [10]
prevent, prevenire *preh-veh-nee'-reh*
previous, precedente *preh-cheh-den'-teh*
price, prezzo *pret'-tsoh* [38]
priest, prete *preh'-teh*
principal, principale *preen-chee-pah'-leh*
prison, prigione (f) *pree-joh'-neh*
prisoner, prigioniero *pree-joh-nyeh'-roh*
private, privato *pree-vah'-toh*
prize, premio *preh'-myoh*
probable, probabile *proh-bah'-bee-leh*
probably, probabilmente *proh-bah-beel-men'-teh*
problem, problema (m) *proh-bleh'-mah*
produce *v.*, produrre *proh-door'-reh*
production, produzione (f) *proh-doo-tsyoh'-neh*
profession, professione (f) *proh-fes-syoh'-neh*
professor, professore (m) *proh-fes-soh'-reh*
profit, profitto *proh-feet'-toh*
program *n.*, programma (m) *proh-grahm'-mah*
progress *n.*, progresso *proh-gres'-soh*
promenade, passeggiata *pahs-sej-jah'-tah*
promise *n.*, promessa *proh-mes'-sah*
prompt, pronto *pron'-toh*
pronunciation, pronunzia *proh-noon'-tsyah*
proof, prova *proh'-vah*
proper, appropriato *ahp-proh-pree-yah'-toh*
property, proprietà *proh-pree-eh-tah'*
proposal, proposta *proh-pos'-tah*
proprietor, proprietario *proh-pree-eh-tah'-ree-yoh*
prosperity, prosperità *proh-speh-ree-tah'*
protect, proteggere *proh-tej'-jeh-reh*
protection, protezione (f) *proh-teh-tsyoh'-neh*
protestant, protestante *proh-tes-tahn'-teh*
proud, orgoglioso *ohr-gohl-yoh'-zoh*

provide, provvedere *prov-veh-deh'-reh*
province, provincia *proh-veen'-chah*
provincial, provinciale *proh-veen-chah'-leh*
provision, disposizione (f) *dees-poh-zee-tsyoh'-neh*
prune, prugna secca, prugna *proon'-yah sek'-kah, proon'-nyah*
public, pubblico *poob'-blee-koh*
publish, pubblicare *poob-blee-kah'-reh*
pull *v.*, tirare *tee-rah'-reh*
pump, pompa *pom'-pah*
punish, punire *poo-nee'-reh*
pupil, alunno *ah-loon'-noh*
purchase *n.*, compera *kom'-peh-rah*
purchase *v.*, comprare *kom-prah'-reh*
pure, puro *poo'-roh*
purple, porpora *por'-poh-rah*
purpose *n.*, scopo *skoh'-poh*
purse, borsa *bor'-sah*
purser, commissario *kom-mees-sah'-ree-yoh*
push *v.*, spingere *speen'-jeh-reh*
put, mettere *met'-teh-reh* [74]

quality, qualità *kwah-lee-tah'*
quantity, quantità *kwahn-tee-tah'*
quarrel *n.*, alterco *ahl-ter'-koh*
quarrel *v.*, litigare *lee-tee-gah'-reh*
quarter *adj. & n.*, quarto *kwahr'-toh*
queen, regina *reh-jee'-nah*
question *n.*, domanda *doh-mahn'-dah*
quick, rapido, veloce *rah'-pee-doh, veh-loh'-cheh*
quickly, rapidamente *rah-pee-dah-men'-teh*
quiet, quieto, silenzioso *kwee-eh'-toh, see-len-tsyoh'-zoh* [38]
quite, molto, del tutto *mol'-toh, del toot'-toh*

radio, radio (f) *rah'-dyoh*

railroad, ferrovia *fer-roh-vee'-yah*

railroad car, vagone (m), carrozza *vah-goh'-neh, kahr-rot'-tsah*

railroad station, stazione ferroviaria *stah-tsyoh'-neh fer-roh-vee-yah'-ree-yah* [45, 82]

rain *n.,* pioggia *pyoj'-jah* [7]

rain *v.,* piovere *pyoh'-veh-reh* [102] **it's raining,** piove *pyoh'-veh*

rainbow, arcobaleno *ahr-koh-bah-leh'-noh* [7]

raincoat, impermeabile (m) *eem-per-meh-ah'-bee-leh* [8]

raise *v.,* sollevare *sol-leh-vah'-reh*

rapidly, rapidamente *rah-pee-dah-men'-teh*

rare, raro *rah-roh*

rash *n.,* eruzione cutanea (f) *eh-roo-tsyoh'-neh koo-tah-neh'-ah*

raspberry, lampone (m) *lahm-poh'-neh*

rate, tariffa *tah-reef'-fah*

rather, piuttosto, abbastanza *pyoot-tos'-toh, ahb-bahs-tahn'-tsah*

raw, crudo *kroo'-doh*

razor, rasoio *rah-zoh'-yoh*

razor blade, lametta (per la barba) *lah-met'-tah (per lah bahr'-bah)*

reach *v.,* raggiungere *rahj-joon'-jeh-reh*

read, leggere *lej'-jeh-reh*

ready, pronto *pron'-toh* [75]

real, vero *veh'-roh*

really, veramente *veh-rah-men'-teh*

rear, di dietro *dee dyeh'-troh*

reason *n.,* ragione (f) *rah-joh'-neh*

reasonable, ragionevole *rah-joh-neh'-voh-leh*

receipt, ricevuta *ree-cheh-voo'-tah* [32]

receive, ricevere *ree-cheh'-veh-reh*

recent, recente *reh-chen'-teh*

reception desk, ricevimento *ree-cheh-vee-men'-toh*

recognize, riconoscere *ree-koh-noh'-sheh-reh*

recommend, raccomandare *rahk-koh-mahn-dah'-reh* [50]

reconfirm [a flight], riconfirmare *ree-kon-feer-mah'-reh* [89]

recover, guarire *gwah-ree'-reh*

red, rosso *ros'-soh*

reduce, ridurre *ree-door'-reh*

reduction, riduzione (f) *ree-doo-tsyoh'-neh*

refreshments, rinfreschi (m, pl) *reen-fres'-kee*

refund *v.*, rimborsare *reem-bohr-sah'-reh*

refuse *v.*, rifiutare *ree-fyoo-tah'-reh*

region, regione (f) *reh-joh'-neh*

register *n.*, registro *reh-jees'-troh*

register [a letter], raccomandare *rahk-koh-mahn-dah'-reh*; [at a hotel], iscriversi sul registro *ees-kree'-vehr-see sool reh-jees'-troh*

regret *v.*, dispiacersi *dees-pyah-chehr'-see*

regular, regolare *reh-goh-lah'-reh*

regulation, regolamento *reh-goh-lah-men'-toh*

relative [kin], parente (m) *pah-ren'-teh*

religion, religione (f) *reh-lee-joh'-neh*

remark *n.*, osservazione (f) *os-ser-vah-tsyoh'-neh*

remember, ricordarsi di *ree-kor-dahr'-see dee*

remove, rimuovere *ree-mwoh'-veh-reh*

renew, rinnovare *reen-noh-vah'-reh*

rent *v.*, affittare *ahf-feet-tah'-reh*

repair *v.*, riparare *ree-pah-rah'-reh*

repeat *v.*, ripetere *ree-peh'-teh-reh* [11]

replace [put back], ricollocare *ree-kol-loh-kah'-reh*

reply *n.*, risposta *rees-pos'-tah*

republic, repubblica *reh-poob'-blee-kah*

request *v.*, chiedere *kyeh'-deh-reh*

rescue *v.*, salvare *sahl-vah'-reh*

reservation, prenotazione (f) *preh-noh-tah-tsyoh'-neh*

reserve *v.*, prenotare, riservare *preh-noh-tah'-reh, ree-zer-vah'-reh* [54]

reserved, riservato *ree-zer-vah'-toh*

residence, residenza *reh-zee-den'-tsah*
resident, residente *reh-zee-den'-teh*
responsible, responsabile *reh-spon-sah'-bee-leh*
rest *n.*, riposo *ree-poh'-zoh*
rest *v.*, riposarsi *ree-poh-zahr'-see*
restaurant, ristorante (m) *rees-toh-rahn'-teh* [38, 48]
restless, irrequieto *eer-reh-kwee-eh'-toh*
rest room, gabinetto *gah-bee-net'-toh*
result *n.*, risultato *ree-zool-tah'-toh*
return *v.*, ritornare, tornare *ree-tohr-nah'-reh, tohr-nah'-reh*
return ticket, biglietto di ritorno *beel-yet'-toh dee ree-tohr'-noh*
review *n.*, rivista *ree-vees'-tah*
reward, ricompensa *ree-kom-pen'-sah*
rib, costola *kos'-toh-lah*
ribbon, nastro *nahs'-troh*
rice, riso *ree'-zoh*
rich, ricco *reek'-koh*
ride *n.*, corsa, passeggiata *kor'-sah, pahs-sej-jah'-tah* [45]
right [correct], corretto *kor-ret'-toh* **to be right,** aver ragione *ah-vehr' rah-joh'-neh* [12] **all right,** molto bene, va bene *mol'-toh beh'-neh, vah beh'-neh*
right [direction], a destra *ah des'-trah*
ring *n.*, anello *ah-nel'-loh*
ring *v.*, suonare *swoh-nah'-reh* [44]
ripe, maturo *mah-too'-roh*
rise *v.*, sorgere *sor'-jeh-reh*
river, fiume (m) *fyoo'-meh* [101, 102]
road, strada, cammino *strah'-dah, kahm-mee'-noh* [75]
roast, arrosto *ahr-rohs'-toh*
rob, rubare *roo-bah'-reh* [15]
robber, ladro *lah'-droh*
rock, roccia *roch'-chah*
roof, tetto *tet'-toh*
roll [bread], panino *pah-nee'-noh*

roll *v.*, rotolare *roh-toh-lah'-reh*

room [of a house], stanza, camera *stahn'-tsah, kah'-meh-rah* [7]; [in a hotel], camera *kah'-meh-rah* [37, 38, 48]

rope, corda *kor'-dah*

rose, rosa *roh'-zah*

rouge, rossetto *ros-set'-toh*

rough, ruvido, aspro *roo'-vee-doh, ahs'-proh*

round, rotondo *roh-ton'-doh*

round trip, andata e ritorno *ahn-dah'-tah eh ree-tor'-noh* [84]

royal, reale *reh-ah'-leh*

rubber, gomma *gom'-mah*

rude, rude, rozzo, sgarbato *roo'-deh, rot'-tsoh, zgahr-bah'-toh*

rug, tappeto *tahp-peh'-toh*

ruin *v.*, rovinare *roh-vee-nah'-reh*

rum, rum (m) *room*

run *v.*, correre *kor'-reh-reh*

runway, pista *pees'-tah* [90]

sad, triste *trees'-teh*

safe, sicuro *see-koo'-roh*

safety pin, spillo di sicurezza *speel'-loh dee see-koo-ret'-tsah*

sail *v.*, navigare, veleggaiare, partire *nah-vee-gah'-reh, veh-lej'-jah-reh, pahr-tee'-reh* [86]

sailor, marinaio *mah-ree-nah'-yoh*

saint, santo *sahn'-toh*

salad, insalata *een-sah-lah'-tah*

sale, vendita *ven'-dee-tah* [68] **for sale**, da vendere *dah ven'-deh-reh*

salesgirl, venditrice (f) *ven-dee-tree'-cheh*

salesman, commesso, venditore *kom-mes'-soh, ven-dee toh'-reh*

salmon, salmone (m) *sahl-moh'-neh*

salt, sale (m) *sah'-leh*
same, stesso *stes'-soh*   **the same as,** lo stesso come *loh stes'-soh ko'-meh*
sample *n.,* campione (m) *kahm-pyoh'-neh*
sand, sabbia *sahb'-byah*
sandwich, panino imbottito *pah-nee'-noh eem-bot-tee'-toh*
sanitary, sanitario *sah-nee-tah'-ree-yoh*
sanitary napkin, pannilino igienico *pahn-nee-lee'-noh ee-jyeh'-nee-koh*
satin, raso *rah'-zoh*
satisfactory, soddisfacente *sod-dees-fah-chen'-teh*
satisfied, soddisfatto *sod-dees-faht'-toh*
satisfy, soddisfare *sod-dees-fah'-reh*
Saturday, sabato *sah'-bah-toh*
sauce, salsa *sahl'-sah*
saucer, piattino *pyaht-tee'-noh*
sausage, salsiccia *sahl-seech'-chah*
save, risparmiare *rees-pahr-myah'-reh*; [rescue], salvare *sahl-vah'-reh*
say, dire *dee'-reh* [11]
scale, bilancia *bee-lahn'-chah*
scar *n.,* cicatrice (f) *chee-kah-tree'-cheh*
scarce, scarso *skahr'-soh*
scarcely, appena *ahp-peh'-nah*
scare *v.,* spaventare *spah-ven-tah'-reh*
scarf, sciarpa *shahr'-pah*
scenery, paesaggio *pah-eh-zahj'-joh*
scent *n.,* promfumo, fiuto *proh-foo'-moh, fyoo'-toh*
schedule *n.,* orario *oh-rah'-ree-yoh*
school, scuola *skwoh'-lah*
science, scienza *shyen'-tsah*
scientist, scienziato *shyen-tsyah'-toh*
scissors, forbici (f, pl) *for'-bee-chee*
scratch *n.,* graffio *grahf'-fyoh*
sculpture, scultura *skool-too'-rah*

sea, mare (m) *mah'-reh*

seafood, pesce e frutti di mare *peh'-sheh eh froot'-tee dee mah'-reh*

seagull, gabbiano *gahb-byah'-noh*

seam, cucitura *koo-chee-too'-rah*

seaport, porto di mare *por'-toh dee mah'-reh*

search *v.,* cercare *cher-kah'-reh*

seasick, soffrendo mal di mare *sof-fren'-doh mahl dee mah'-reh* [88]

season, stagione (f) *stah-joh'-neh*

seat, posto *pos'-toh* [84]

second, secondo *seh-kon'-doh* **second class,** seconda classe *seh-kon'-dah klahs'-seh* [83, 87]

secret *adj. & n.,* segreto *seh-greh'-toh*

secretary, segretario *seh-greh-tah'-ree-yoh*

section sezione (f) *seh-tsyoh'-neh*

see, vedere *veh-deh'-reh* [3, 7, 99]

seem, sembrare, parere *sem-brah'-reh, pah-reh'-reh*

select *v.,* scegliere *shehl'-yeh-reh*

selection, selezione (f) *seh-leh-tsyoh'-neh*

self, stesso, stessa *stes'-soh, stes'-sah*

sell, vendere *ven'-deh-reh* [67, 70]

send, mandare, spedire *mahn-dah'-reh, speh-dee'-reh* [13, 70]

sensible, ragionevole *rah-joh-neh'-voh-leh*

separate *adj.,* separato *seh-pah-rah'-toh*

separate *v.,* separare *seh-pah-rah'-reh*

September, settembre (m) *set-tem'-breh*

series, serie (f) *seh'-ree-yeh*

serious, serio *seh'-ree-yoh*

servant, servo, domestico *ser'-voh, doh-mes'-tee-koh*

serve *v.,* servire *ser-vee'-reh* [50, 64, 90]

service, servizio *ser-vee'-tsee-yoh*

service charge, spese di servizio (f, pl) *speh'-zeh dee ser-vee'-tsee-yoh*

set [fixed], fissato *fees-sah'-toh*

set [place] *v.*, mettere *met'-teh-reh*
seven, sette *set'-teh*
seventeen, diciassette *dee-chahs-set'-teh*
seventh, settimo *set'-tee-moh*
seventy, settanta *set-tahn'-tah*
several, parecchi *pah-rek'-kee*
severe, severo *seh-veh'-roh*
sew, cucire *koo-chee'-reh*
shade, ombra *om'-brah*
shampoo, shampoo *shahm-poo'*
shape *n.*, forma *for'-mah*
share *v.*, condividere *kon-dee-vee'-deh-reh*
shark, pescecane (m) *peh-sheh-kah'-neh*
sharp, affilato, aguzzo *ahf-fee-lah'-toh, ah-goot'-tsoh*
shave *v.*, farsi la barba, radersi *fahrsee lah bahr'-bah, rah'-der-see*
shaving cream, crema per la barba *kreh'-mah per lah bahr'-bah*
she, ella, essa, lei *el'-lah, es'-sah, leh'-ee*
sheep, pecora *peh'-koh-rah*
sheet [of paper], foglio *fohl'-yoh* bedsheet, lenzuolo *len-tswoh'-loh*
shellfish, frutti di mare *froot'-tee dee mah'-reh*
shelter, rifugio *ree-foo'-joh*
sherry, vino di Xeres *vee'-noh dee sheh'-rehs*
shine *v.*, lustrare *loos-trah'-reh*
ship *n.*, nave (f) *nah'-veh* [86, 87]
ship *v.*, spedire *speh-dee'-reh* [70]
shirt, camicia *kah-mee'-chah* [40, 69]
shiver *v.*, tremare *treh-mah'-reh*
shock *n.*, colpo *kol'-poh*
shoe, scarpa *skahr'-pah* [69]
shoelace, laccio *lahch'-choh*
shoeshine, lustro di scarpe *loos'-troh dee skahr'-peh*
shoestore, calzoleria *kahl-tsoh-leh-ree'-yah*
shoot *v.*, sparare *spah-rah'-reh*

shop *n.*, negozio *neh-goh'-tsyoh*

shop: to go shopping, fare delle compere *fah'-reh del'-leh kom'-peh-reh* [62]

shopping center, centro di compere *chen'-troh dee kom'-peh-reh* [102]

shore, sponda, riva *spon'-dah, ree'-vah*

short, corto *kor'-toh* [68, 69]

shorts, mutande (f, pl) *moo-tahn'-deh*

shoulder, spalla *spahl'-lah*

show *n.*, spettacolo *spet-tah'-koh-loh*

show *v.*, mostrare *mos-trah'-reh* [13, 67, 95]

shower [bath], doccia *doch'-chah* [37]

shrimp, gambero *gahm'-beh-roh*

shut *adj.*, chiuso *kyoo'-zoh*

shut *v.*, chiudere *kyoo'-deh-reh*

shy, timido *tee'-mee-doh*

sick, ammalato *ahm-mah-lah'-toh* [92]

side, lato, fianco *lah'-toh, fyahn'-koh*

sidewalk, marciapiede (m) *mahr-chah-pyeh'-deh*

sight, vista *vees'-tah*

sightseeing, girare per vedere le curiosità *jee-rah'-reh per veh-deh'-rah leh koo-ree-yoh-zee-tah'* [98]

sign *n.*, insegna *een-sehn'-yah*

sign *v.*, firmare *feer-mah'-reh* [32]

signature, firma *feer'-mah*

silence, silenzio *see-len-tsee'-yoh*

silent, silenzioso *see-len-tsee-yoh'-zoh*

silk, seta *seh'-tah*

silly, sciocco, stolto *shok'-koh, stol'-toh*

silver, argento *ahr-jen'-toh*

similar, simile *see'-mee-leh*

simple, semplice *sem'-plee-cheh*

since, da, dacchè, siccome *dah, dahk-keh', seek-ko'-meh*

sing, cantare *kahn-tah'-reh*

single, singolo *seen'-goh-loh*

sir, signore *seen-yoh'-reh*

sister, sorella *soh-rel'-lah* [3]
sit, sedersi *seh-dehr'-see* [100]
situation, situazione (f) *see-too-ah-tsyoh'-neh*
six, sei *seh'-ee*
sixteen, sedici *seh'-dee-chee*
sixth, sesto *ses'-toh*
sixty, sessanta *ses-sahn'-tah*
size, misura, *mee-zoo'-rah* [67]
skilled, skillful, abile *ah'-bee-leh*
skin, pelle (f) *pel'-leh*
skirt, gonna, gonnella *gon'-nah, gon-nel'-lah* [68]
skull, cranio *krah'-nee-yoh*
sky, cielo *chyeh'-loh*
sleep *n.,* sonno *son'-noh*
sleep *v.,* dormire *dor-mee'-reh* [96]
sleeve, manica *mah'-nee-kah* [69]
slice *n.,* fetta *fet'-tah*
slice *v.,* affettare *ahf-fet-tah'-reh*
slight, leggero *lej-jeh'-roh*
slip [garment], sottogonna *sot-toh-gon'-nah*
slip *v.,* scivolare *shee-voh-lah'-reh*
slippers, pantofole (f, pl) *pahn-toh'-foh-leh*
slippery, sciovoloso, sdruccievole *shee-voh-loh'-zoh, zdrooch-chyeh'-voh-leh* [75]
slow, lento *len'-toh*
slowly, lentamente, adagio, pian piano *len-tah-men'-teh, ah-dah'-joh, pyahn pyah'-noh* [11, 45]
small, piccolo *peek'-koh-loh*
smart, svelto *zvel'-toh*
smell *n.,* odore *oh-doh'-reh*
smell *v.,* odorare *oh-doh-rah'-reh*
smile *n.,* sorriso *sor-ree'-zoh*
smile *v.,* sorridere *sor-ree'-deh-reh*
smoke *n.,* fumo *foo'-moh*
smoke *v.,* fumare *foo-mah'-reh* [89, 96]
smooth, liscio *lee'-shoh*

snack, spuntino *spoon-tee'-noh*

snow, neve (f) *neh'-veh* **it's snowing,** nevica *neh'-vee-kah*

so, così *koh-see'* **so as,** così che *koh-see' keh* **so that,** affinchè *ahf-feen-keh'*

soap, sapone (m) *sah-poh'-neh* [40]

social, sociale *soh-chah'-leh*

sock, calzino *kahl-tsee'-noh*

soda, soda *soh'-dah*

soft, soffice, morbido, molle *sof'-fee-cheh, mor'-bee-doh, mol'-leh*

sold, venduto *ven-doo'-toh*

solid, solido *soh'-lee-doh*

some, del, della, dei *del, del'-lah, deh'-ee*

somehow, in qualche modo *een kwahl'-keh moh'-doh*

someone, qualcuno *kwahl-koo'-noh*

something, qualche cosa, qualcosa *kwahl'-keh ko'-zah, kwahl-ko'-zah*

sometimes, qualche volta *kwahl'-keh vol'-tah*

somewhere, in qualche luogo *een kwahl'-keh lwoh'-goh*

son, figlio *feel'-yoh* [3]

song, canzone (f) *kahn-tsoh'-neh*

soon, fra poco *frah poh'-koh*

sore *adj.*, dolente *doh-len'-teh*

sore throat, mal di gola *mahl dee goh'-lah*

sorrow, afflizione (f) *ahf-flee-tsyoh'-neh*

sorry: to be sorry, dispiacere a, rincrescere a *dees-pyah-cheh'-reh ah, reen-kreh'-sheh-reh ah* [3] **I'm sorry,** mi dispiace, mi rincresce *mee dees-pyah'-cheh, mee reen-kreh'-sheh*

sort, sorta *sor'-tah*

soul, anima *ah'-nee-mah*

sound *n.*, suono *swoh'-noh*

soup, zuppa, minestra *dzoop'-pah, mee-nes'-trah* [54]

sour, agro, acido *ah'-groh, ah'-chee-doh* [52]

south, sud (m) *sood*

southeast, sud-est *sood-est'*

southwest, sud-ovest *sood-oh'-vest*

souvenir, ricordo *ree-kor'-doh*

space, spazio *spah'-tsee-yoh*

speak, parlare *pahr-lah'-reh* [43] **do you speak English?**
  parla Lei inglese? *pahr'- leh'-ee een-gleh'-zeh*

special, speciale *speh-chah'-leh*

specialty, specialità *speh-chah'-lee-tah*

speed, velocità *veh-loh-chee-tah'* [75]

spell *v.,* sillabare, scrivere *seel-lah-bah'-reh, skree'-veh-reh*

spend, spendere *spen'-deh-reh*

spicy, piccante *peek-kahn'-teh*

spinach, spinaci (m, pl) *spee-nah'-chee*

spine, spina dorsale *spee'-nah dor-sahl'-leh*

splendid, splendido *splen'-dee-doh*

spoiled, guasto *gwah'-toh*

spoon, cucchiaio *kook-kee-yah'-yoh* [55]

spot *n.,* macchia *mahk'-kee-yah*

sprain *n.,* storta *stor'-tah*

spring [season], primavera *pree-mah-veh'-rah*

spring [water], sorgente (f) *sor-jen'-teh*

springs [of a car], molla *mol'-lah*

square *adj.,* quadrato *kwah-drah'-toh*

square [public], piazza *pyaht'-tsah* [100]

stairs, scala *skah'-lah*

stamp, francobollo *frahn-koh-bol'-loh* [40]

stand *v.,* stare in piedi *stah'-reh een pyeh'-dee*

star, stella *stel'-lah* [7]

starch, amido *ah'-mee-doh*

start *n.,* principio *preen-chee'-pyoh*

start *v.,* cominciare *kom-een-chah'-reh*

state, stato *stah'-toh*

stateroom, cabina *kah-bee'-nah*

station, stazione (f) *stah-tsyoh'-neh* [82] ·

statue, statua *stah'-too-ah*

stay *v.,*   stare, rimanere *stah'-reh,   ree-mah-neh'-reh*
  [16, 38, 39, 94]

steak, bistecca *bees-tek'-kah*
steal *v.*, rubare *roo-bah'-reh* [15]
steel, acciaio *ahch-chah'-yoh*
steep, erto *er'-toh*
step, passo, gradino *pahs'-soh, grah-dee'-noh*
stew, stufato *stoo-fah'-toh*
steward, cameriere (m) *kah-mee-ree-yeh'-reh* [87]
stick *n.*, stecco *stek'-koh*
stiff, rigido *ree'-jee-doh*
still [quiet], tranquillo *trahn-kweel'-loh*
still [yet], tuttavia, eppure *toot-tah-vee'-yah, ep-poo'-reh*
sting *n.*, puntura *poon-too'-rah*
sting *v.*, pungere *poon'-jeh-reh*
stockings, calze (f, pl) *kahl'-tseh*
stolen, rubato *roo-bah'-toh*
stomach, stomaco *stoh'-mah-koh* [92]
stone, pietra *pyeh'-trah*
stop *n.*, fermata *fer-mah'-tah*
stop *v.*, fermarsi *fer-mahr'-see* [14, 45 46, 84]
store *n.*, negozio *neh-goh'-tsyoh* [62, 99]
storey, piano *pyah'-noh*
storm, tempesta, temporale (m) *tem-pes'-tah, tem-poh-rah'-leh*
story, storia *stoh'-ree-yah*
straight, diritto *dee-reet'-toh*
straight ahead, sempre diritto *sem'-preh dee-reet'-toh* [45]
strange, strano *strah'-noh*
stranger, straniero *strah-nyeh'-roh*
strawberry, fragola *frah'-goh-lah*
stream, corrente (f) *kor-ren'-teh*
street, strada, via *strah'-dah, vee'-yah* [37, 46, 100, 101]
streetcar, tranvia *trahn-vee'-yah*
strength, forza *for'-tsah*
string, spago *spah'-goh*
strong, forte *for'-teh*
structure, struttura *stroot-too'-rah*

student, studente *stoo-den'-teh*

study *v.*, studiare *stoo-dee-yah'-reh*

style, stile (m) *`stee'-leh*

suburb, sobborgo, dintorni (m, pl) *sob-bor'-goh, deen-tor'-nee*

succeed [follow], seguire *seh-gwee'-reh;* [attain one's goal], riuscire *ree-oo-shee'-reh*

success, successo *sooch-ches'-soh*

such, tale *tah'-leh*

suddenly, improvvisamente, ad un tratto *eem-prov-vee-zah-men'-teh, ahd oon traht'-toh*

suffer, soffrire *sof-free'-reh*

sufficient, sufficiente *soof-fee-chyen'-teh*

sugar, zucchero *dzook'-keh-roh* [51, 52]

suggest, suggerire *sooj-jeh-ree'-reh*

suggestion, suggerimento *sooj-jeh-ree-men'-toh*

suit, vestito, abito *vest-tee'-toh, ah'-bee-toh*

suitcase, valigia *vah-lee'-jah* [39]

summer, estate (f) *es-tah'-teh*

sun, sole (m) *soh'-leh* [6]

sunburned, bruciato dal sole *broo-chah'-toh dahl soh'-leh*

Sunday, domenica *doh-meh'-nee-kah*

sunglasses, occhiali da sole *ok-kyah'-lee dah soh'-leh*

sunny, soleggiato *soh-lej-jah'-toh*

supper, cena *chen'-nah* [51]

sure, sicuro *see-koo'-roh*

surface, superficie (f) *soo-per-fee'-chyeh*

surprise *n.*, sorpresa *sor-preh'-zah*

surprise *v.*, sorprendere *sor-pren'-deh-reh*

suspect *v.*, sospettare *soh-spet-tah'-reh*

suspicion, sospetto *sos-pet'-toh*

sweater, maglione di lana (m) *mahl-yoh'-neh dee lah'-nah* [8]

sweep, spazzare, scopare *spaht-tsah'-reh, skoh-pah'-reh*

sweet, dolce *dol'-cheh*

swim, nuotare *nwoh-tah'-reh* [102]

swollen, gonfiato *gon-fyah'-toh*
sword, spada *spah'-dah*

table, tavola *tah'-voh-lah* [50, 54, 57, 87]
tablecloth, tovaglia *toh-vahl'-yah* [56]
tailor, sarto *sahr'-toh*
take, prendere *pren'-deh-reh* [51, 67]   **take off,** decollare
   deh-kol-lah'-reh [89]
talk, parlare *pahr-lah'-reh*
tall, alto *ahl'-toh*
tank, serbatoio *ser-bah-toh'-yoh*
taste *n.,* gusto *goos'-toh*
taste *v.,* assaggiare, gustare, saporare *ahs-saj-jah'-reh,*
   goos-tah'-reh, sah-poh-rah'-reh
tax *n.,* tassa *tahs'-sah*
taxi, tassì *tahs-see'* [44]
tea, tè (m) *teh* [53]
teach, insegnare *een-sehn-yah'-reh*
teacher, maestro *mah-ehs'-troh*
tear [drop], lagrima *lah'-gree-mah*
tear *v.,* strappare *strahp-pah'-reh*
teaspoon, cucchiaino *kook-kyah-ee'-noh*
teeth, denti (m, pl) *den'-tee*
telegram, telegramma (m) *teh-leh-grahm'-mah*
telephone, telefono *teh-leh'-foh-noh* [41]
telephone booth, cabina telefonica *kah-bee'-nah teh-leh-*
   foh'-nee-kah
telephone operator, telefonista, centralino *teh-leh-foh-*
   nees'-tah, chen-trah-lee'-noh
television, televisione (f) *teh-leh-vee-zyoh'-neh*
tell, dire, raccontare *dee'-reh, rahk-kon-tah'-reh* [13, 46]
temperature, temperatura *tem-peh-rah-too'-rah*
temple, tempio *tem'-pyoh*
temporary, provvisorio *prov-vee-zoh'-ree-yoh*
ten, dieci *dyeh'-chee*
tent, tenda *ten'-dah*

tenth, decimo *deh'-chee-moh*
test, prova *proh'-vah*
than, di, che *dee, keh*
thank, ringraziare *reen-grah-tsyah'-reh* **thank you,** grazie *grah'-tsee-yeh*
thankful, grato *grah'-toh*
that *adj.,* quello, quel, quell', quella *kwel'-loh, kwel, kwel, kwel'-lah*
that *conj.,* che *keh*
that *pron.,* quello, quella *kwel'-loh, kwel'-lah*
the, il, la, l', lo i, le, gli *eel, lah, l, loh, ee, leh, lyee*
theater, teatro *teh-ah'-troh* [101]
theft, furto *foor'-toh*
their, loro *loh'-roh*
theirs, loro *loh'-roh*
them, loro, li, le *loh'-roh, lee, leh*
then, allora *ahl-loh'-rah*
there *adv.,* lì, là, ci *lee, lah, chee* **there is, there are,** c'è, ci sono *cheh, chee soh'-noh*
therefore, perciò *per-choh'*
thermometer, termometro *ter-moh'-meh-troh*
these *adj., & pron.,* questi, queste *kwes'-tee, kwes'-teh*
they, loro, essi, esse *loh'-roh, es'-see, es'-seh*
thick, spesso *spes'-soh*
thigh, coscia *koh'-shah*
thin, sottile, magro *sot-tee'-leh, mah'-groh*
thing, cosa *ko'-zah*
think, pensare *pen-sah'-reh*
third, terzo *ter'-tsoh*
thirst, sete *seh'-teh*
thirsty: to be thirsty, aver sete *ah-vehr' seh'-teh* [47, 48]
thirteen, tredici *treh'-dee-chee*
thirty, trenta *tren'-tah*
this *adj.,* questo, questa, quest' *kwes'-toh, kwes'-tah, kwest*
this *pron.,* questo, questa *kwes'-toh, kwes'-tah*

those *adj.*, quelli, quelle, quegli, quei *kwel'-lee, kwel'-leh, kwel'-yee, kweh'-ee*

those *pron.*, quelli, quelle *kwel'-lee, kwel'-leh*

thoroughfare, strada principale *strah'-dah preen-chee-pah'-leh*

thousand, mille *meel'-leh*

thread, filo *fee'-loh* [70]

three, tre *treh*

throat, gola *goh'-lah*

through *prep.*, per, attraverso *per, aht-trah-ver'-soh*

through [finished], finito *fee-nee'-toh*

throw, lanciare, gettare *lahn-chah'-reh, jet-tah'-reh*

thumb, pollice (m) *pol'-lee-cheh*

thunder, tuono *twoh'-noh*

Thursday, giovedì *joh-veh-dee'*

ticket, biglietto *beel-yet'-toh* [83, 85, 89]

ticket office, sportello dei biglietti *spor-tel'-loh deh'-ee beel-yet'-tee* [83]

tie [bind], legare *leh-gah'·reh*

tight, stretto *stret'-toh* [69]

tighten, stringere *streen'-jeh-reh*

till, fino a, finchè *fee'-noh ah, feen-keh'*

time, tempo, volta *temp'-poh, vol'-tah* **what time is it?** che ora è? *keh oh'-reh eh* **on time**, a tempo *ah tem'-poh*

timetable, orario *oh-rah'-ree-yoh* [83]

tip [money], mancia *mahn'-chah* [57]

tire [of a car], gomma, pneumatico *gom'-mah, pneh-oo-mah'-tee-koh* [74]

tire *v.*, stancarsi *stahn-kahr'-see*

tired, stanco *stahn'-koh* [100]

to, a, ad *ah, ahd*

toast, pane tostato *pah'-neh tos-tah'-toh*

tobacco, tabacco *tah-bahk'-koh* [34]

tobacconist, tabaccaio *tah-bahk-kah'-yoh*

today, oggi *oj'-jee* [5, 99]

toe, dito del piede *dee'-toh del pyeh'-deh*

together, insieme *een-syeh'-meh*

toilet, gabinetto *gah-bee-net'-toh*

toilet paper, carta igienica *kahr'-tah ee-jyeh'-nee-kah*

tomato, pomodoro *poh-moh-doh'-roh*

tomorrow, domani *doh-mah'-nee* [3, 6, 40, 96]

tongue, linqua *leen'-gwah* [95]

tonight, questa notte, stasera *kwes'-tạh not'-teh, stah-seh'-rah*

tonsils, tonsille (f, pl) *ton-seel'-leh*

too [excessive], troppo *trop'-poh;* [also], anche *ahn'-keh*

tooth, dente (m) *den'-teh*

toothache, dolor di denti *doh-lohr' dee den'-tee*

toothbrush, spazzolino da denti *spaht-tsoh-lee'-noh dah den'-tee*

toothpaste, pasta dentifricia *pahs'-tah den-tee-free'-chah*

top, cima *chee'-mah*

torn, strappato *strahp-pah'-toh*

total, totale *toh-tah'-leh*

touch *v.*, toccare *kok-kah'-reh*

tough, duro, resistente *doo'-roh, reh-zees-ten'-teh*

tour, giro *jee'-roh* [99, 102]

tow, rimorchiare *ree-mor-kyah'-reh*

toward, verso *ver'-soh*

towel, asciugamano *ah-shoo-gah-mah'-noh* [40]

town, città *sheet-tah'*

toy, giocattolo *joh-kaht'-toh-loh*

toy shop, negozio di giocattoli *neh-goh'-tsyoh dee joh-kaht'-toh-lee*

trade, commercio *kom-mer'-choh*

traffic, traffico *trahf'-fee-koh*

train, treno *treh'-noh* [15, 82, 83, 84, 85]

transfer *v.*, trasferire *trahs-feh-ree'-reh* [46]

translate, tradurre *trah-door'-reh*

translation, traduzione (f) *trah-doo-tsyoh'-neh*

translator, traduttore (m), traduttrice (f) *trah-doot-toh'-reh, trah-doot-tree'-cheh*

transmission, trasmissione (f) *trahz-mees-syoh'-neh*

transportation, trasporto *trahs-por'-toh*

travel v., viaggiare *vyahj-jah'-reh*

traveler, viaggiatore (m) *vyahj-jah-toh'-reh*

traveler's check, assegno di viaggio *ahs-sehn'-yoh dee vyahj'-joh* [31]

tray, vassoio *vahs-soh'-yoh*

tree, albero *ahl'-beh-roh*

trip, viaggio *vyahj'-joh* [88]

tropical, tropicale *troh-pee-kah'-leh*

trousers, pantaloni (m, pl) *pahn-tah-loh'-nee*

truck, camione (m) *kah-myoh'-neh*

true, vero *veh'-roh*

trunk, baule (m) *bah-oo'-leh*

truth, verità *veh-ree-tah'*

try v., tentare, cercare di *ten-tah'-reh, cher-kah'-reh dee*

try on, provarsi *proh-vahr'-see* [67, 69]

Tuesday, martedì *mahr-teh-dee'*

turn n., giro, voltata *jee'-roh, vol-tah'-tah*

turn v., girare *jee-rah'-reh* [45]

twelve, dodici *doh'-dee-chee*

twenty, venti *ven'-tee*

twice, due volte *doo'-eh vol'-teh*

twin beds, letti gemelli *let'-tee jeh-mel'-lee*

two, due *doo'-eh*

ugly, brutto *broot'-toh*

umbrella, ombrello *om-brel'-loh* [6]

uncle, zio *dzee'-yoh*

uncomfortable, scomodo *skoh'-moh-doh*

unconscious, inconscio, privo di sensi *een-kon'-shoh, pree'-voh dee sen'-see*

under *prep.*, sotto *sot'-toh*
underneath *prep.*, disotto *dee-sot'-toh*
undershirt, camiciola *kah-mee-choh'-lah*
understand, capire *kah-pee-reh* [11]
underwear, maglia *mahl'-yah*
undress *v.*, svestirsi *zves-teer'-see*
unequal, ineguale *een-eh-gwah'-leh*
unfair, ingiusto *een-joos'-toh*
unfortunate, sfortunato *sfor-too-nah'-toh*
unhappy, infelice *een-feh-lee'-cheh*
unhealthy, malsano *mahl-sah'-noh*
United States, Stati Uniti (m, pl) *stah'-tee oo-nee'-tee*
university, università *oo-nee-ver-see-tah'*
unless, a meno che *ah meh'-noh keh*
unlucky, sfortunato *sfor-too-nah'-toh*
unpack, disfare le valige, sballare *dees-fah'-reh leh vah-lee'-jeh, zbahl-lah'-reh*
unpleasant, spiacevole *spyah-cheh'-voh-leh*
unsafe, non sicuro *non see-koo'-roh*
until, fino a, finchè *fee'-noh ah, feen-keh'*
untrue, falso *fahl'-soh*
unusual, insolito *een-soh'-lee-toh*
up, su *soo*
upper, superiore *soo-peh-ree-yoh'-reh*
upstairs, sopra *soh'-prah*
urgent, urgente *oor-jen'-teh*
us, noi, ci *noy, chee*
use *n.*, uso *oo'-zoh* [34]
use *v.*, usare *oo-zah'-reh*
useful, utile *oo'-tee-leh*
useless, inutile *een-oo'-tee-leh*
usual, usuale, solito *oo-zoo-ah'-leh, soh'-lee-toh*

vacant, libero *lee'-beh-roh*
vacation, vacanze (f, pl) *vah-kahn'-tseh*

vaccination, vaccinazione (f) *vahch-chee-nah-tsyoh'-neh*
valuable, prezioso, di valore *preh-tsyoh'-zoh, dee vah-loh'-reh*
value *n.,* valore (m) *vah-loh'-reh*
vanilla, vaniglia *vah-neel'-yah*
variety, varietà *vah-ree-eh-tah'*
veal, vitello *vee-tel'-loh*
vegetables, legumi (m, pl) *leh-goo'-mee*
very, molto *mol'-toh*
vest, panciotto *pahn-chot'-toh*
victim, vittima *veet'-tee-mah*
view *n.,* veduta, vista *veh-doo'-tah, vees'-tah* [37]
village, villaggio *veel-lahj'-joh*
vinegar, aceto *ah-cheh'-toh*
visa, visto *vees'-toh*
visit *n.,* visita *vee'-zee-tah*
visit *v.,* visitare *vee-zee-tah'-reh* [99, 101, 103]
voice, voce (f) *voh'-cheh*
volcano, vulcano *vool-kah'-noh*
voyage *n.,* viaggio *vyahj'-joh*

waist, vita *vee'-tah*
wait *v.,* aspettare *ahs-pet-tah'-reh* [12, 45]
waiter, cameriere (m) *kah-meh-ree-yeh'-reh* [50, 56]
waiting room, sala d'aspetto *sah'-lah dahs-pet'-toh* [85]
waitress, cameriera *kah-meh-ree-yeh'-rah* [50]
wake up, svegliare, svegliarsi *zvehl-yah'-reh, zvehl-yahr'-see*
walk *n.,* passeggiata *pahs-sej-jah'-tah*
walk *v.,* camminare *kahm-mee-nah'-reh* [100]
wall, muro, parete (f) *moo'-roh, pah-reh'-teh*
wallet, portafogli (m) *por-tah-fohl'-yee*
want *v.,* volere *voh-leh-reh* **I want,** voglio *vohl'-yoh*
warm, caldo *kahl'-doh* [52, 55]
warn, avvertire *ahv-ver-tee'-reh*

warning, avvertimento, avvertenza *ahv-ver-tee-men'-toh, ahv-ver-ten'-tsah*

wash *v.*, lavare *lah-vah'-reh* [40, 74]

wasp, vespa *ves'-pah*

watch *n.*, orologio *oh-roh-loh'-joh*

watch *v.*, guardare, osservare *gwahr-dah'-reh, os-ser-vah'-reh*

water, acqua *ahk'-kwah* [8, 51, 74]

waterfall, cascata *kahs-kah'-tah.*

wave [ocean], onda *on'-dah*

way [manner], maniera, modo *mah-nyeh'-rah, moh'-doh*

we, noi *noy*

weak, debole *deh'-boh-leh*

wear *v.*, indossare, portare *een-dos-sah'-reh, por-tah'-reh*

weather, tempo *tem'-poh* [5, 6, 7]

Wednesday, mercoledì *mer-koh-leh-dee'*

week, settimana *set-tee-mah'-nah* [38, 39]

weigh, pesare *peh-zah'-reh*

weight, peso *peh'-zoh*

welcome *n.*, benvenuto *ben-veh-noo'-toh*

well, bene *beh'-neh*   **well done** [food], ben cotto *ben kot'-toh*

well [for water], pozzo *pot'-tsoh*

west, ovest (m) *oh'-vest*

wet, bagnato *bahn-yah'-toh* [75]

what *interr.*, che? che cosa? *keh, keh ko'-zah*   **what else?** che altro? *keh ahl'-troh?*

wheel, ruota *rwoh'-tah*

when, quando *kwahn'-doh*

whenever, ogni volta che *ohn'-yee vol'-tah keh*

where, dove *do'-veh*   **where is, where are,** dov'è, dove sono *do-ve', do'-veh soh'-noh*

wherever, dovunque *do-voon'-kweh*

which *interr.*, quale? *kwah'-leh*

while, mentre *men'-treh*

whip *n.*, frusta *froos'-tah*
white, bianco *byahn'-koh* [69]
who *interr.*, chi? *kee*
who [*rel.*,] che *keh*
whole, intero *een-teh'-roh*
whom *interr.*, chi? *kee*
whose *interr.*, di chi? *dee kee*
why *interr.*, perchè? *per-keh'*
wide, largo *lahr'-goh* [69, 75]
width, larghezza *lahr-get'-tsah*
wife, moglie (f) *mohl'-yeh* [2]
wild, selvaggio *sel-vahj'-joh*
willing, disposto a *dees-pos'-toh ah*
win *v.*, vincere *veen'-cheh-reh*
wind, vento *ven'-toh* [6, 7]
window, finestra *fee-nes'-trah* [39, 84]
windshield, parabrezza *pah-rah-bret'-tsah* [76]
wine, vino *vee'-noh* [55]   **red wine**, vino rosso *vee'-noh ros'-soh*   **white wine**, vino bianco *vee'-noh byahn'-koh*
wing, ala *ah'-lah*
winter, inverno *een-ver'-noh*
wipe, pulire *poo-lee'-reh* [76]
wise, saggio *sahj'-joh*
wish *n.*, desiderio, augurio *deh-zee-deh'-ree-yoh, ow-goo'-ree-yoh*
wish *v.*, desiderare *deh-zee-deh-rah'-reh* [44, 64]
with, con *kon*
without, senza *sen'-tsah*
woman, donna *don'-nah* [10]
wonderful, meraviglioso *meh-rah-veel-yoh'-zoh*
wood, legno *lehn'-yoh*
woods, bosco *bos'-koh*
wool, lana *lah'-nah*
word, parola *pah-roh'-lah*
work *n.*, lavoro *lah-voh'-roh*
work *v.*, lavorare *lah-voh-rah'-reh*

world, mond *moon'-doh*
worried, preoccupato *preh-ok-koo-pah'-toh*
worse, peggiore, peggio *pej-joh'-reh, pej'-joh*
worth, valore *vah-loh'-reh*
wound [injury], ferita *feh-ree'-tah*
wrap *v.,* avvolgere *ahv-vol'-jeh-reh* [70]
wrist, polso *pol'-soh*
wristwatch, orologio da polso *oh-roh-loh'-joh dah pol'-soh*
write, scrivere *skree'-veh-reh* [13, 30]
writing, scrittura *skreet-too'-rah*
wrong: to be wrong, aver torto *ah-vehr' tor'-toh* [12]

x ray, raggi x *rahj'-jee eh-kees*

yard, cortile (m) *kor-tee'-leh*
year, anno *ahn'-noh* [89]
yellow, giallo *jahl'-loh*
yes, sì *see*
yesterday, ieri *yeh'-ree* [6]
yet, ancora *ahn-koh'-rah*
you, Lei, voi, tu *leh'-ee, voy, too*
young, giovane *joh'-vah-neh*
your, yours, suo, sua, vostro, vostra, tuo, tua *soo'-oh, soo'-ah vos'-troh, vos'-trah, too'-oh, too'-ah*

zero, zero *dzeh'-roh*
zipper, chiusura lampo *kyoo-zoo'-rah lahm'-poh*

CONVERSION TABLES

Length
1 centimetro (cm) = 0.39 inch
1 metro (m) = 39.36 inches
1 chilometro (km) = 0.62 mile
1 inch = 2.54 cm.
1 foot = 0.30 m.
1 mile = 1.61 km.

Weight
1 grammo (gm) = 0.04 ounce
1 kilo (kg) = 2.20 pounds
1 ounce = 28.35 gm.
1 pound = 453.59 gm.

Volume
1 litro = 0.91 dry quart
1 litro = 1.06 liquid quarts
1 pint liquid = 0.47 liter
1 US quart liquid = 0.95 liter
1 US gallon = 3.78 liters

Temperature

Celsius (°C):	−17.8	0	10	20	30	37	37.8	100
Fahrenheit (°F):	0	32	50	68	86	98.6	100	212